My Life and
the Overthrow of the
Persian Peacock Throne

Siamak A. Adibi, MD, PhD

LT. Christian Allaid
best regards
Siamak Adibi

New Publishing Partners
Washington, DC

Copyright © Siamak A. Adibi, MD, PhD, 2015

Published by New Publishing Partners
2510 Virginia Avenue
Suite 702N
Washington, DC 20037
www.npp-publishing.com

ISBN-13: 978-0-9882500-2-4
ISBN-10: 0988250020

Cover design, book design, and photo editing by Deborah Lange

The cover photo shows the Amir Ahmad fortress in the Caucuses. It was built by Siamak Adibi's ancestor and is an international heritage site.

To Joan Adibi, my wife and partner for over half a century, who has given me three wonderful children and who has greatly helped me to succeed in my profession

Contents

Acknowledgments

I would like to thank several people who greatly helped me to write this book.

The writing of this book required typing and I never learned how to type. Mary Ann Krupper, who was my secretary for many years and who could read my handwriting, agreed to type my manuscript on her computer. I am greatly indebted to her.

I am also grateful that my wife, Joan Adibi, took the time and attention to edit the manuscript and to enter the photographs in the computer. That required skill and expertise that I did not possess. I appreciate her patience and loving support.

Lastly, I would like to thank Audrey Wolf and Debbie Lange for agreeing to publish my book.

Notations

Throughout the text, numbers in parentheses refer to the references listed at the end of the book.

Preface

This memoir is a thoughtful discussion of current tensions between Iran and the United States and a firsthand account of how the changes have affected the author.

The story is brought to light by my husband, a man who was born in Iran and who lived in Iran for 18 years before he emigrated all alone to the United States. He comes from an illustrious family of generals and members of the royal court and diplomats who have been associated with the kings of Iran for centuries.

Siamak Adibi is a poet and a scientist who is eminently qualified to analyze the historic events leading to this stand-off, both from the perspective of an Iranian and an American citizen. In America during his career he became a world-renowned Professor of Medicine who published and spoke on the basic science of nutrition. His base has been Pittsburgh, Pennsylvania, where he lives, where he worked and where he raised his family. And from there he traveled widely, including periodic visits back to Iran.

He has always been interested and active in world affairs. And it is through his accomplishments in medicine that he hoped he could bridge the gap between his two countries. The story is compelling from his perspective as a headstrong, first-born son who took the bold step of leaving his family of origin and making it on his own in a foreign country. His reason for coming to this country was driven by his attraction to the principles of democracy. And when he left Iran, there was a real possibility that there was going to be a constitutional monarchy with a democratic prime minister, named Mossadegh.

The feeling of being let down takes on new meaning when he discusses the reasons behind the ouster of the Shah of Iran, the rise to power of Ayatollah Khomeini, the hostage crisis and Islamic Revolution and the controversy relating to nuclear enrichment.

Joan Adibi

Introduction

Because I was born in Iran (previously called Persia), I am often asked "Why is there such animosity between Iran and America?" Before answering this question, I need to discuss the story of my life which was profoundly affected by this animosity. My personal story includes first growing up and being shaped by Iran, and then moving to America, where I embraced all that the United States of America stood for. The story of my life in Iran and America will enable the readers of my book to know how I came to love both countries and why now why I feel disheartened by both governments.

As the first-born son, the "crown prince," I quickly displayed my determination to get what I wanted. Later, as a teen-ager, against the family's wishes, I decided to travel alone over 12,000 miles to America to study medicine. My strong will and initiative has allowed me to overcome all obstacles and to establish a national and international reputation for making significant contributions to medical science. These contributions are reviewed in the following pages.

All of this happened while I was busy trying to advance the field of medicine in both countries. When the Shah (King) was in power in the early 1970's, I accepted the invitation to become the Imperial Chief of Medicine. In 1979 I was ready to move my family to Iran and nearly got caught in the bloody revolution of the Iranians. A decade later after the Islamic clergies came to power, I accepted the invitation to serve as advisor to the National Academy of Science of the Islamic Republic of Iran. Regrettably, my intention to help was opposed by ultra conservative Islamic Clergies.

The relevance of the story of my growing up in Iran is to show how deep was my love for the country and its people and how unhappy I am for Iranian failure to achieve democracy.

When I left Iran, I was so optimistic that Iran might become a democratic kingdom. My desire for a kingdom was based on a thousand years of history of great Persian kings and my ancestors being deeply involved in working with the kings in governing and defending the empire.

The story of my maturation in America shows the growth of my love for America. I was proud of becoming also an American citizen and experiencing its political freedoms. My adopted new country appeared to be unique in the world by using its resources to help other countries, without exploiting them. America has helped countries like Japan and Germany, countries that were our bitter enemies in WWII. But when I learned how America in a covert operation destroyed the aspirations of my hero, Dr. Mossadegh, my idealistic view of America was shattered. Dr. Mossadegh was the only leader that truly brought democracy to Iran and freed the country from the exploitations of the British colonial mercenaries. To put the nationalistic goals of Mossadegh in perspective, I have recounted how his vision arose from several thousand years of Iran's history.

In the last chapter, by looking back and incorporating my unique experiences, I answer the frequently asked question, "Why for more than half a century has a once very friendly relationship between Iran and America turned hostile?

Siamak A. Adibi, MD, PhD

Part 1: Growing up in Iran

1 The City of My Birth

I was born in 1932 into an old and prominent family in Tehran, which has been the capital of the country since 1795. Apparently, my birth was a great source of joy for my parents because they had waited a long time to have a son. In Persian culture, a son is considered to be similar to a crown prince. The crown prince serves an important function. He is expected to keep the family name and traditions alive after they have passed away. Furthermore, he is to look after them when they become old and disabled.

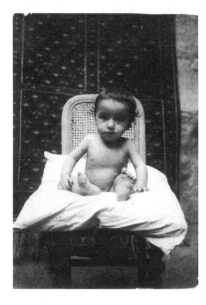

My picture when I was a few months old, showing me in a serious mood, probably already thinking about the responsibilities of being a crown prince.

When I was growing up, Tehran was a beautiful city. There were wide tree-lined boulevards under the shadow of the tall snow-covered Alborz mountains. The cold crystal mountain water flowed as streams through some of these boulevards. The most fashionable street, called Lalezar, was located in central Tehran. It was in walking distance from our house and I liked to walk there often. My attraction to it were all of the movie theaters, and the best pastry shops and the cafes were located there. My favorite reason for going to pastry shops was to eat cream puffs and for going to the cafes was to eat salami sandwiches, called kolbas in Persian.

Initially, when I was very young, my father insisted that I go with a servant. As a teenager, I went alone.

In addition to beauty, Tehran had a combination of Western and Eastern cultures. The north was under the influence of Western culture and the rich people and the south under Eastern culture and the poor people. This was reflected in the design of buildings and the living styles of people. This contrast made Tehran an interesting city.

The population was rather small. As a result the streets were not crowded and were kept clean. It was great fun to walk and to look at stores and people. To get around Tehran was quite easy by public transportation, including buses and horse and carriages. In fact, since my brother-in-law had a stable of racing horses, I would go horseback riding with him through the streets of Tehran and its outskirts for pleasure.

In the south of Tehran, you could often see caravans of camels bringing fresh farm products from the villages. For bargain shopping, you would also go to southern Tehran, where the picturesque bazaars were located. For shopping for fancy and stylish clothing, you would go north to the expensive stores.

Tehran, in contrast to many other Middle Eastern cities, enjoyed full social freedom. For example, the women did not have to wear chador or hijab (face cover). In fact they were banned in the 1930s by the order of Reza Shah who was against the Islamic laws. The men and women of northern Tehran were commonly dressed in the latest western fashion and walked, either hand in hand, or arm in arm. In fact, my sister, Roshan, who was eight years older, used to wear the most fashionable décolleté dresses which made me uncomfortable to go shopping with her, because men would stare at her.

Also there was no restriction on food such as pork or alcoholic beverages like wine and beer, which are forbidden by the Islamic laws. As far as pork is concerned, in my childhood my favorite lunch was to go to an Armenian restaurant and have a salami (kolbas in Persian) sandwich. The Armenian kolbas was far tastier than American salami. When I visited later after the Islamic takeover of Iran, I could no longer find any Armenian restaurants and so was deprived of having my favorite lunch. As far as alcoholic beverages are concerned, I did not drink alcohol at all in my childhood.

I shall never forget my only crime in life, my recent arrest in the Tehran airport by the Islamists for carrying a bottle of wine in my suitcase. Whenever I went to Tehran, my sister served me wine with dinner that she got in the black market. On one occasion I planned to go for a few days to the Island of Kish in the Persian Gulf. My sister gave me a bottle of wine to take with me. She said that I will be safe if I hide it in my suitcase. Unfortunately, she was not aware of the airport having a new scanner that can detect a wine bottle even in a suitcase. As soon as airport security discovered a wine bottle in my suitcase they arrested me for violating Islamic law. They handcuffed me and took me to the airport criminal court to see a judge. When we got there the judge had just left the court. The security officer told me that I have to wait until the judge returns. This took several hours of waiting because the judge had to have his lunch and after-lunch nap followed by his afternoon Islamic prayers.

When the judge returned I defended myself by telling him that my doctor has told me to drink a couple of glasses of red wine per day as a treatment for my heart disease and that he could call my doctor in Pittsburgh. He rejected my defense and fined me a large sum of Iranian money. I had no choice but to pay the fine. I was relieved that they let me go free and that I was able to join my wife who all day was seated in the airport worrying about me. Although we missed our scheduled flight, we got lucky to find a late flight that would take us to the Island of Kish. After my scary experience, we enjoyed a few days of biking and swimming on desolate and beautiful beaches of the Kish. The weather was like a hot summer while the weather in Tehran was like a cold winter.

The ruling Islamic clergies must not be aware that wine drinking is an ancient Iranian custom. In fact, the evidence suggests that wine was first produced in Iran. In the Tehran Glassware Museum there is a beautiful wine glass that is around 5,000 years old. In fact, pots for making grape wine that are over 7,000 years old have been recently discovered in the Zagros Mountains in Iran.

Outside of Iran, people around the world still enjoy the descendent of Iranian wine called "Shiraz."

Except for the summers, I lived in the family house in Tehran. The house was in a key section of Tehran, only a block away from the House of Parliament. The house was large and built in the style of Persian architecture. For example, it had a grand entrance hall with a large Persian designed chandelier. In the center of the hall, under the chandelier, there was a small pond with a water fountain. The walls of the entrance hall were covered with hand crafted turquoise mosaics that you would see in ancient mosques. Some of the mosaics had incorporated pictures of my grandfather and father. From the entrance hall you could enter a large reception hall or walk through a big door to an open courtyard. On the three sides of the courtyard, there were living rooms, bedrooms, dining room, balconies, kitchen, bathroom, and servant quarters. All were built separate from each other, but connected through the courtyard.

There was a sizable garden in the middle of the courtyard. Besides trees and flowers, the garden contained a swimming pool with a statue of a man holding a fountain in the middle of the pool. The garden also contained a circle of flowers with a pond and a fountain in the middle. In the good weather the courtyard was used by family members and guests to sit outside and to enjoy eating and drinking. In the winter, my younger brother and I would use the courtyard for snow fights. After the fights we would treat ourselves to fresh snow mixed with fruit syrups.

One spring day a friend of my father brought him a gift of a live baby deer that he had captured on his farm. My father's plan was to use the baby deer to make a venison feast for the family dinner party. I put up a great fight that I wanted to keep the baby deer as my pet. He could not resist my demand and finally agreed. It was the most unusual sight for people to see a deer in a formal garden in the heart of the city. Unknown to me the baby deer grew to be a very large animal and caused great damage to our beautiful garden. Even more serious was his growing attraction to people. Because of my great friendship with him, he lost his fear of people and when a guest entered our garden, he would jump on the guest by putting up his two front legs on each shoulder of the guest and begin to kiss. This became intolerable to my family and I had to agree to his sacrifice, a painful decision for me.

The Tehran that I grew up in has radically changed. It is now enormously congested with people because of enormous expansion of the city and its surroundings. The population when I was growing up was less than a million. Now it is over 14 million people. It is very hard to move around the city because of traffic jams everywhere. The old architectures have been largely replaced with apartment buildings and high rises. Because of pollution the air is difficult to breathe. The old western style of dress has been replaced with the Islamic dress code. This is more severe in women than in men. You will not find any restaurant that will serve you pork or alcoholic beverages.

In contrast to other seasons, the summer season in Tehran is unbearable. It is hot sun every day and temperature during the day is usually above 100°F. Fortunately, Tehran is surrounded by a tall mountain called Alborz, which offers a very nice refuge from the summer heat in Tehran. Some affluent people, like my relatives, had summer villas in the Alborz mountain area called Shemiran. It was about an hour drive from the center of Tehran. The king's summer palace was close to our villas. In fact, on occasions, I would see the crown prince riding his horse in front of our villa. The summer villas of my relatives had magnificent gardens and swimming pools. I spent most of my childhood summers in these villas playing with my cousins during the day and sleeping outside under a clear sky at night. The sky was always full of stars and when the moon was full, everywhere was very bright and magical. Therefore, my happiest memories of childhood are my summers in Shemiran.

The area between Tehran and Shemiran, except for a few oases, was all a beautiful desert. The desert, like Tehran, is now completely covered with buildings, shops, and malls. The desert and most of the villas in Shemiran all have disappeared and replaced with apartments and condominiums. Roadside merchants and vendors have trashed the beautiful streams coming down the Alborz Mountains with food stands. Even the magnificent garden of the old royal summer palace has been turned into a restaurant. It has become depressing to me to visit the city of my birth that once I loved and of which I have fond memories. Even more depressing to me than congestion and the buildup of the city is to see that even the social freedom that people enjoyed during the Pahlavi kings has been abolished by the ruling conservative clergies. For example, in the severe heat of the summer, I was not allowed to wear shorts or a short-sleeved shirt; like the women, I had to cover myself when I went out.

2   The Country of My Birth and Its History

The country of my birth, called Iran by some and Persia by others, is one of the oldest civilizations in the world, several thousand years old. It was the world's first super power. Since the ancient days, the country has had a vast plural society, including all major religions, such as Zoroastrianism, Judaism, Christianity, and Islam and all major races, including white and black, Aryans and Semitics. The history is very long and complex and there are many books available for a comprehensive review of Persian history. Therefore, I am presenting a very brief review derived from a few recent sources (1-3).

Iran currently has an area of 628,000 square miles, which makes it the 16th largest country in the world, roughly the size of the U.S. east of the Mississippi. In the north, it is surrounded by the Caspian Sea and Russia and its former republics, in the south by the Persian Gulf and Indian Ocean, in the west by Turkey and Iraq, and in the east by Afghanistan and Pakistan. In ancient times, many of these countries were part of the Persian Empire. Because of these neighboring countries and ocean access, Iran is considered to have a key strategic location.

Although it is not clear how early in human history civilization was developed in Iran, there is evidence that it was over 7,000 years before the Common Era (B.C.E.). The evidence is based on the discovery of artifacts. For examples, in the Tehran National Museum there is a well-preserved hunter who lived around 5,000 years ago.

In the Bronze Age Semitic people called Elamites created a vibrant regional civilization that spread across much of the Iranian plateau. Elam became a full-fledged kingdom by 2700 B.C.E. In the height of their power, one of their kings sacked Babylon and carried off many of its treasures to Iran. Among these was the famous stone pillar inscribed with the legal Code of Hammurabi that is now in the British Museum.

Sometime in 2000 B.C.E., Indo-European tribes of Aryan race began to migrate from central Asia to various locations around the world. A group of them came to the southern Iranian plateau and settled in an area that they called Parsa. The Greek historian Herodotus called it "Persia" and its peoples "Persians." Currently, it is called Fars Province.

The Persians expanded the country they founded to include people like the Elamites, Medes, Babylonians, Lydians, Assyrians, Egyptians, Scythians, Ionians, Parthians, Bactrians, Indians, and Arabs. However, world historians for thousands of years continued to call the country Persia. In 1935, under the insistence of the government, the country became known as Iran. This was done because the kings in the 3rd Century C.E. called the country Iran.

This was done to acknowledge that we were an Aryan Nation composed of many different peoples besides Persians like me.

After migration, the first major cultural contribution of the Persians to the world was the creation of the first monotheistic religion called Zoroastrianism. Before the prophet Zarathustra (Greeks called him Zoroaster), people worshipped a number of gods and goddesses who represented nature, such as sun, moon, rain, wind, etc. Zoroaster proclaimed the existence of a single supreme god by the name of Ahura Mazda, who commanded people "to have good will," "good thoughts," and "good deeds." God's instructions to Zoroaster form the doctrines of the religion that are recorded in a book called Avesta. A key doctrine is that human life is a struggle between good and evil. There is also a god by the name of Ahriman who encourages people to do evil. It is man's free will and responsibility to avoid Ahriman. There will be a last day of judgment when a messiah will come to raise the dead and to pass those who committed sins through holy fire to burn their sins. For this reason the Zoroastrians keep a fire (the symbol of Ahura Mazda) always lit in their temples. Zoroastrianism deeply influenced the subsequent religions like Judaism, Christianity, and Islam. The influence of Zoroaster has continued to recent times like the philosophy of Nietzsche and the musical composition of Richard Strauss.

The second global impact of the Persians was the rise of Cyrus the Great as their king in 600-530 B.C.E. He was a descendent of a legendary Persian hero by the name of Hakamanesh. The Greeks called him Achaemenes. He built the biggest empire in human history, extending from India and China to across the Middle East and Central Asia to across North Africa and extending to European continent. Unlike subsequent invaders like Arabs and Mongols, Cyrus did not allow the massacre of conquered people and respected their culture and religion. In fact, when he captured Babylon, he freed all the Jews held captives there, sent them to their homes in Jerusalem, and rebuilt their temple. For these thoughtful and kind acts, the prophet Isaiah called him a "messiah."

Even American presidents, like Thomas Jefferson and Harry Truman, were impressed with the noble acts of Cyrus. For example, after creating the state of Israel, Harry Truman, in a gathering of Jewish leaders at the Jewish Theological Seminary, compared himself to Cyrus the Great. The most historic relic of Cyrus is his Cylinder in the British museum. It is the first (2000 years before the Magna Carta) proclamation of human rights, freedom of religion, equality of races, and justice for all.

Cyrus enjoyed expanding his empire, but was not much interested in managing it. This task became the main objective of Darius, who became king of Achaemenids after Cyrus and ruled between 522 and 486 B.C.E. He declared "Ahura Mazda bestowed the kingdom upon me." Darius was the real architect of the Persian Empire. He put it in order and perfected the institutions to maintain it. For example, he developed an effective administration system for his incredibly vast empire. He divided it into 20 territories. The home territory (Pars or Persia) was under the direct rule of the king, but others were under the jurisdiction of an official called "Satrap." The Satrap, acting like a governor or a local king, was usually a member of the royal family or a member of the Persian nobility. Satrapies, through inspectors, were under the eyes and ears of the king to insure they governed justly and did not grow to be too powerful or independent. Darius also built roads to allow travel through the empire and to connect the 20 satrapies. The royal couriers carried oral and written messages by galloping in relays between the rest stations on the royal roads. Their goal was to cover 1,600 miles in 9 days.

Darius also built a majestic building complex in Persepolis to serve as a ceremonial center and a place to receive royal subjects who were offering gifts. The subjects came from all the corners of the Persian Empire and were of different races, religions and cultures. Finally, Darius revolutionized the economy by placing it on a silver and gold coinage system and promoting trades through the far reaches of the empire.

After the assassination of Philip, his son Alexander became the king of Macedonia (now part of Greece). Because the power of Achaemenids after Darius had declined, Alexander saw an opportunity to conquer the biggest empire. Therefore, during 300 B.C.E., he attacked Persia and in a series of battles, he routed the Persian army, razing Zoroastrian temples, massacring the Zoroastrian priests, and burning the magnificent capital of Achaemenids in Persepolis. During the course of his attack, he realized that the Persian culture is far richer than that of his native Macedonia causing him to fall in love with the Persian culture. He began to copy Persian dress, court rituals and etiquettes. He even went further by marrying the daughter of the defeated Persian king and commanding his generals and soldiers to marry Persian women. Finally, Alexander proclaimed his wish that the Persians and Macedonians should rule together in harmony as an imperial power. However, before he could fulfill his wish, he died in 323 B.C.E. in Babylon. One of Alexander's generals (Seleucus) decided to stay in Persia and bring the Greek culture to the empire. The Seleucids ruled to around 230 B.C.E. when the Parthians, a branch of Persian tribes, drove them out of the country. Parthians restored the country and its Persian language, which had been heavily influenced by the Greeks. Zoroastrianism once again became the religion of the most of the people. In fact, historians consider Parthians responsible for resurrecting a second Persian empire. The Parthians enjoyed a relative period of tranquility until the first century C.E.

Then the Roman emperors and generals became interested in conquering Persian territories. The group included notables such as Nero, Augustus, Marcus Aurelius, Marc Antony (the lover of Cleopatra), and Julius Caesar. In fact, Brutus and Cassius, after killing Julius Caesar, turned to Persians to save them, but they refused.

In the beginning of the 3rd Century C.E., people became disenchanted with Parthians and revolted. Ardeshir, a descendant of the legendary hero Sasan, took advantage of this to become the ruler of Pars (Persia), which was the home province of Achaemenids. In 224 C.E., he overthrew the last Parthian king and established the Sassanid dynasty, which lasted for 400 years. The Sassanids established the third and last Persian Empire within the frontiers achieved by the Achaemenids. The Sassanid kings, like the legendary Khosrow Anushirvan (528-579), put their main efforts on advancing the living and culture of citizens and on maintaining a civil and responsible government. For examples, they built new irrigations to improve farming and agricultural productions. They expanded urban life by building new cities. They greatly improved the system of justice and the maintenance of law and order.

The Sassanid kings built a great university with a renowned medical school in Gundishapur. They assembled great teachers from around the world to make it truly an international center for teaching the science and practice of medicine among other disciplines. The medical center included the first teaching hospital in the world. It was staffed by physicians, nurses, and pharmacists and housed a huge medical library containing 400,000 books. The most famous book, *The Canon of Medicine* written by IbuSina, was translated into all major languages and was used to teach medical students worldwide until the mid-17th century. Finally, to impress the citizens and visitors, they built grand royal palaces with magnificent crowns and regalia, and monuments with carvings of their glories. The main problem of Sassanians, like

Parthians before them, was meaningless wars with Romans, and subsequently with Byzantine emperors without either side ever achieving a decisive victory. Even the Sassanian King Shapur's capturing the emperor Valerian in the Battle of Antioch did not help to stop the fighting. These wars drained the military and financial resources of both Persian and Byzantine empires to make them easy prey for conquest by the Bedouin Arabs in the 7th Century.

With the demise of Sassanids in 642 C.E. for about nine centuries (7th to 16th), the Persian Empire went through a series of invasions by Arabs, Mongols, and Turks, resulting in loss of independence. These invasions were accompanied with massacres of people and destructions of cities. The Persians tried to endure the invasion by teaching the invaders how to govern the conquered lands and become civilized. The Arabs gave up the desert life and merged into Persian culture. The Persian poets and scholars kept their language alive despite a great deal of mixing with the languages of the invaders. Among the invaders, the Arabs had the most profound and lasting effects on the Persian culture, some of which have continued to the present day. After two centuries of occupation, the Arabs succeeded to convert most of the Persians from Zoroasterism to Islam and changed their alphabet to Arabic. As a result people often confuse the Persians with the Arabs although they were distinctly different people. The Persians were Aryans and the Arabs were Semitic people with a different language and culture. Many Persian scholars, for political reasons, had Arabic names, resulting in being identified as "Arab" by historians.

After several centuries of occupation, in 1501 the Safavids, a native Iranian dynasty, came to power by forming the 4th empire after the Persians. The Safavid order, probably of Kurdish origin, was founded in the 14th Century by Shaykh Safi al Din, who was a Sufi Moslem. In 1501 under their leader Ismail, they captured a major Iranian city by the name of Tabriz to become their capital. Ismail was proclaimed the Shah (King) of Iran. The Safavids formed a strong central government and declared the Shia Islam as the official religion of the kingdom. This probably was intended to separate the Iranians from the Arabs, who are mostly followers of Sunni Islam. The Sunnis believe that the message of God was completed with the prophet Mohammed, while the Shias believe the religious mission of Mohammed was continued through twelve imams who were his descendants. Furthermore, the last imam has disappeared to reappear on earth on the last day for final judgment. Imam is the man who stands before the world to lead it in divine path.

The Savafids reached their height of glory during the reign of Shah Abbas (1587-1629), who was the greatest of all the Safavid rulers. As will be reviewed in the next chapter, he was the king who appointed a distant ancestor of mine to become the satrapy of Caucuses and, in particular, the Protector of the Silk Road through Caucuses. This road was very important for trading between Persia and Europe.

The main adversary of Shah Abbas was the Ottoman emperor. They had many battles, but Shah Abbas succeeded in retaining territories like Caucasus, Iraq, and Afghanistan. He moved the capital to a city called Isfahan. With exquisite architectures he made the Isfahan one of the most magnificent and beautiful cities in the world. The centerpiece of his well-planned city was an immense rectangular park that allowed activities like parades and polo playing.

Shah Abbas recognized the advantages of foreign alliances and international trades. Therefore, he opened Iran to the outside world by welcoming many Europeans who were merchants, diplomats, and missionaries to come to Iran. He brought many skilled Armenians to Isfahan to modernize his army.

Between 1507 and 1515, the Portuguese, in search of influence in the Indian Ocean, occupied the Iranian island of Hormuz in the straits between the Persian Gulf and the Indian Ocean. Since Shah Abbas did not have a navy strong enough to get rid of the Portuguese he made a deal with the English to do it for him. Recently the island of Hormuz has become a strategic concern of Western and U.S. powers for shipment of oil.

After Shah Abbas, the Safavid rulers became weak and ineffectual, resulting in decline of Safavid Empire and finally being overthrown by Nader Khan Afshar. The last Safavid king appointed Nader Khan, a brilliant general, as his military commander. As a general he defeated the Ottomans and Russians forcing them to withdraw their forces from the Caucuses. For these military actions he used my ancestral fortress in the Caucuses for his headquarters.

In 1736 Nader Khan called himself king. In 1739 he attacked India. His interest did not appear to be territorial but taking the Indian treasures. He extracted a large amount of cash and jewels, including the famous Koh-e-Noor diamond and the jewel-covered Peacock Throne from the rulers of India. The Iranians have continued to benefit from the treasures that Nader Shah brought from India because they are still used to back Iranian currency. The past several Persian kings had used the Peacock Throne for their coronations. Unfortunately, in contrast to his brilliance in military undertakings, Nader Shah showed very little interest in the state matters. This, together with his harsh manners, convinced his officers that he had gone insane, so they killed him.

At the end of the 18th Century, Agha Mohammad Khan, a member of Ghajar (in the west it is call Qajar) tribe formed an army and captured Tehran. He then assumed the title of Shah and made Tehran his capital. He founded the Ghajar dynasty that lasted over 100 years (1795-1925). The Ghajars were of Turkish origin and several centuries earlier had migrated from central Asia to Iran to become Persians. The Ghajar dynasty was the worst dynasty Iran has ever had. The kings were brutal and kept the country backward. They had very little skill in running the country. On several occasions their prime minister turned out to be a visionary reformer with plans to bring order and progress to the country. On each of these occasions, the king became jealous and fearful of his prime minister and had him killed. For example, Naser al-Din Shah had a very brilliant and reform-minded prime minister by the name of Amir Kabir. The king became fearful of the rising reputation of Amir Kabir for modernizing the Country so he ordered his assassination.

In the 19th Century, when the western countries were advancing their democracy and science and technology, the Persian kings were busy building their massive harems and amusing themselves.

As a result they lost all the Caucuses and Central Asia territories to Russia and Afghanistan to the British. In fact, the British and Russians got together and divided Persia into two spheres for their influence and exploitation: north for Russia, south for England. These two countries by the use of military threats and bribing the kings and their officials kept the country under their control. The discovery of oil in the south of Persia in 1908 further increased England's appetite for exploiting resources of Persia.

Finally, in the late 19th Century, the Persians began to express anger at their ineffectual and corrupt rulers who had brought oppression, economic hardship, and disorder to the country. People demanded a curb on the royal authority, the establishment of the rule of law, freedom of expression, and the elimination of foreign influences. This led to the first constitutional revolution in the Middle East. In 1906 the king was forced to agree to create a constitution. An elected assembly was convened which drew up a constitution that provided for strict limitation of the royal power and an elected parliament with wide powers to represent the people, and a government with a cabinet subject to confirmation by the parliament. The constitution was essentially similar to those in operation in European kingdoms with democracy. Unfortunately, soon after the establishment of democracy in Iran, the king died. His successors were against democracy; consequently, the parliament was closed a few years after its opening.

After the demise of the spring of democracy the condition of the country further deteriorated. In 1921 a group of Persian Cossacks brigade officers, including my father, under the leadership of a senior officer by the name of Reza Khan, marched into Tehran and seized power. In 1923 the Ghajar king agreed to appoint Reza Khan as the prime minister and go into exile in Europe. This allowed Reza Khan to assume full power of controlling the country and in 1926 becoming king and founder of the Pahlavi dynasty.

To repair all the damages that were done by Ghajar kings, the unifying and modernizing of the country needed a strong and enlightened king. Indeed, Reza Shah met these descriptions. He developed many plans for changing Iran. Although he supported the existence of a parliament, he packed the parliament with his supporters. To strengthen the authority of the central government, he developed a disciplined and well-armed army. With the use of the army he greatly reduced or eliminated the power of the tribal chiefs and put them all under government control. He created a vast system of educational institutions, including primary and secondary schools, and universities, all in the European style. These educational opportunities, together with economic expansion, allowed development of a large middle class in Iran. The quality of life and commerce was advanced by building hospitals, communications systems, new roads, railways, factories, and banking systems.

A major contribution of Reza Shah was to free the educational and social systems of domination and control by the Islamic clergies. For example, he imposed European dress codes on both men and women, opened the schools and jobs to women, and abolished the wearing of the veil. He considered religion as the servant of the state and not vice versa. In fact, he put a lot of effort into bringing back the Persian identity by glorifying the pre-Islamic period. With these accomplishments he made himself a great leader and a popular king.

Unfortunately, as often happens to a ruler with absolute power, he became greedy and cruel. By taking land he became the biggest landlord. He built up an immense personal fortune, allowed no criticism of his rule, and repressed the press. Although he supported the existence of a Parliament, he packed the Parliament with his supporters. He imprisoned or killed many politicians that he did not like. He finally made a fatal misjudgment. He became fed up with the British exploiting his country's wealth (oil) and approached America for help with oil. America did not want to alienate the British and therefore refused to become involved. Reza Shah then became friendly with the Germans for commercial cooperation. When World War II began, England demanded that Reza Shah expel all German citizens from Iran. He refused. When Hitler attacked Russia, Iran was needed for sending war materials to that country. In 1941 England invaded Iran from the south and Russia from the north. In view of Reza Shah's friendly relationship with Germany, he was forced to abdicate and was sent into exile in a British colony in South Africa where he died.

His son ascended to the throne as Mohammed Reza Shah Pahlavi. For the duration of the war, the young king was treated like a hostage of the Allied Forces. The occupation of Iran by the Allied Forces allowed the U.S. to send over several million tons of munitions and other war materials to the Soviet Union.

The king initially ruled democratically. But after the CIA coup removed Mossadegh as prime minister, because he was advocating democracy, the king was persuaded to become an absolute ruler. After 25 years of his ruling, a large majority of people, wanting democracy and improved economic conditions, revolted against him. He was forced to give up his throne and leave the country.

People in search of a loving father figure and savior turned to Ayatollah Khomeini to guide them. He was a religious leader who since 1962 had been the sharpest and most constant outspoken critic of the Shah and his regime. He was forced to flee the country and take exile in the Middle Eastern countries and finally in France. Even in exile he continued to preach to the people in Iran, by sending taped messages to rise against the Shah. People assumed that as a holy man and a religious leader he would safeguard the development of democracy and freedom of expression. Therefore, when he returned from the exile, a very large crowd of people gathered in the airport to greet him. Unfortunately, it turned out that he had the most radical plan for Iran. He cleverly called the revolution Islamic despite the participation of many non-Islamics. He declared he wanted to rule the country as its supreme leader and select a government consisting of mostly Islamic clergies. He rejected the constitutional democracy in favor of religious theocracy using the Islamic laws and customs. He called the country "Islamic Republic of Iran," the first time a country has been called "Islamic Republic."

Khomeini's successor Ayatollah Khamenei has followed vigorously the policies of his predecessor. For example, he has continued to select candidates for the office of president and membership as a deputy in the Parliament. Over 8 years ago, one of his approved candidates for the office of the presidency was Mahmoud Ahmadinejad, who turned out to be a reckless politician.

Under Ahmadinejad the government became more suppressive of the freedom than the previous presidents and he was less capable of managing the country's economy. Therefore, when he ran for a second term election there were many peaceful demonstrations for the election of a moderate reformist candidate. People were greatly angered when Ahmadinejad was declared the winner of the election. When they rose to protest the result of the election , in a "Green Revolution," they were brutally crushed by the revolutionary guard and security forces. It seems as long as these forces remain loyal to the supreme leader, there will not be any possibility of reform or establishment of democracy.

Fortunately, in the last election that took place in June 2013, one candidate (Hassan Rouhani), after being approved by the supreme leader to run for the presidential election, promised if elected he would try to resolve the hostility between Iran and western countries. He won the election by a great margin and people poured out into the streets to celebrate his victory. People believe friendship with the western countries will greatly improve their current economic miseries. This will be further discussed in the last chapter.

3   My Father and His Ancestors

My father's ancestors were Persians who had converted to Sunni Islam in the Middle Ages. In 16th Century the founder of Safavid dynasty (Shah Ismail) declared the Shia Islam as the official religion of Iran. He began to make life difficult for Sunni Moslems. To escape this oppression my ancestors moved to Caucuses and settled in an area close to the Georgian territory. Caucuses extend from the Caspian Sea to the Black Sea and include Georgia, Armenia, and Azerbaijan. They became parts of Persian Empire during the kingdom of Achaemenid (550–330 B.C.E.) and remained so until they were taken by Russia in the 19 Century. The rulers of various parts of the Empire were required to bring gifts to the royal court in Persepolis. According to the Greek historian Herodotus, the Achaemenid kings requested a gift of 100 Georgian girls every four years. The Georgians were considered the most beautiful women in the empire. Actually, from the ancient time there have been many interactions between Persians and Georgians. For example, in the 3rd Century B.C.E., the first Georgian king was Pharnavaz (a Persian name) who was a son of a Persian woman and a follower of Zoroastrianism, which was the Persian religion (4).

Over thousands of years Georgia, like Persia itself, has changed hands. For example, in 1606 Shah Abbas, the great Safavid king, took back Georgia from the Ottomans. To please the European leaders, he allowed Georgia to remain autonomous, but appointed my distant ancestor Amir Ahmad, who was a Satrapi in the Caucuses, to be in charge of the security of the Caucuses, particularly the Silk Road. As discussed in the previous chapter, the position of Satrapi was created by Darius, an Achaemenid king, around 500 B.C.E. to help him to rule the vast Persian Empire. The Silk Road was the major route for allowing trading between Asiatic and European countries for over 2000 years. To be guardian of security in the Caucuses, my ancestor Amir Ahmad built a military base in a region called Qazax-Askipara.

This location allows proximity to Georgia, Armenia, and Azerbaijan. Therefore, it is a good choice for a military base in the Caucuses. The Amir Ahmad military base had great value to the Iranian kings. For example, in the mid-18th Century Nader Shah Afshar used it to drive Ottomans out of Georgia and Armenia and Russians out of Azerbaijan.

After Nader Shah the Ghajar dynasty rose to power in Iran. The founder of Ghajar dynasty was a brutal king and apparently did not like what the Georgians were doing so he attacked Tbilisi and massacred its inhabitants. My ancestors were sharply critical about this and asked the Ottoman emperor for asylum. Apparently, he was very warm and hospitable and happy to have them. In fact, he bestowed upon them the highest honor by giving them the title of "Pasha" meaning next to a shah in importance. Most of my relatives on the father's side call themselves Pashai.

In the early 19th Century, when Iran lost the entire Caucasus to Russia, my ancestor Shah Mohammad Pashai was the head of Caucasus. It is not clear why this ancestor was called shah (king). Probably he was the most powerful ruler among my ancestors and people called him shah. He was a brave king, refused to give up, and kept fighting the Russians. Finally, he was captured by the Russians and put in prison. This ended my ancestors being called royals or satraps (i.e., kings) of the Caucuses.

Apparently, the army of the Shah Mohammad remained loyal to him while he was in prison. They got together and organized a dangerous mission of rescuing him from the prison. They miraculously succeeded in their mission. On their return to their home base, however, they constantly bragged about the bravery of their action. Shah Mohammad became tired of listening to their bragging and expressed the desire to be returned to his prison in Russia. When this was reported to the Czar of Russia, Nikolai I, he was enchanted with the character of my ancestor Shah Mohammad and immediately ordered his release from the prison but with the condition that he be kept under house arrest.

Because Shah Mohammad was Persian, the Persian king, Mohammad Shah Ghajar, asked the Czar to allow Shah Mohammad Pashai and his relatives to immigrate to Tehran sometime around 1840. They were well received in the Royal Court of Ghajar. Through a royal decree his three sons were given high positions in the government. My great grandfather, Ghasem Khan, became the governor of the state of Lorestan and my great grand uncle, Pasha Khan, became the head of Persian imperial guard.

Two years ago I became greatly interested in seeing my ancestral fortress. My wife and my daughter, Jennifer, who speaks fluent Russian, accompanied me. Most of the people in the Caucuses still speak Russian and Jennifer was able to translate our conversations with the people. We flew to Tblisi, which is only 30 minutes away by car from my ancestral place in an area called Askipura. We thought Askipura had become part of Azerbaijan. However, when we went to Azerbaijan Embassy for visas to go there we learned that Askipura has been taken over by Armenia and it is dangerous to go there because of active hostilities between the two countries. We, therefore, returned home after our failed mission. However, I did not give up trying, because the year after I explored the possibility of visiting my ancestral fortress with the

The fortress built in the Caucuses by my ancestor Amir Ahmad. There is a plaque on the wall designating that fortress as an international heritage site (see arrow). This picture was taken many years before I visited the fortress.

The buildings around it, which probably were barracks for soldiers, were all near state of extinction. Our driver told me that the Azeri soldiers had used the fortress to shoot at the advancing Armenian soldiers.

The vista from the fortress was breathtaking by showing a spectacular view of nature, including mountains, lush green valleys, a river and streams.

A recent picture of the Amir Ahmad fortress taken during my visit showing great decay. The plaque designating the international heritage site has disappeared either by theft or by falling down. The Armenian Government has no money to preserve the old historic buildings.

My grandfather, General Adib Nezam. He was both a poet and a general. Therefore, the King gave him the title of Adib Nezam, meaning "military poet." My grandfather was a in the Persian Cossack brigade. The uniform mimics the dress code of the imperial Russian army that were in charge of educating the Persian army during the Ghajar period.

help of Armenians. I was fortunate to find an Armenian driver who was willing to drive me and my wife to Voskepar. The Armenians call Askipura the Voskepar.

The driver had spent his military time in Voskepar fighting the Azeris. Therefore, he was quite familiar with the area. It was an emotional visit to see the Amir Ahmad Fortress. For over 200 years no family member had gone there to visit. It still stands, but has greatly decayed.

My father (Sadegh Khan) was the son of a general who was also a poet. In fact, he was the favorite poet of the Royal Court of Ghajars. They gave him the title of "Adib Nezam." Adib means "man of letters" and Nezam means "military." When in the early 20th Century it became mandatory to have a last name, my father chose the name of "Adibi instead of Pashai, conveying the relation to Adib Nezam.

The General Adib Nezam suffered a terrible accident when riding in his carriage to his office, resulting in serious injuries and great deal of pain. The accident occurred over 100 years ago and at that time, apparently, there were no effective treatments for his injuries and pain. After several years suffering, the general could no longer bear the suffering and committed suicide. My father,

Sadegh Khan, was in the courtyard playing when suddenly he heard a loud sound from his father's room. He rushed to his room to see what had happened. He was horrified to see his father lying on the floor bleeding and his eyes filled with tears.

My father screamed for help, but by the time the servants arrived the general was dead. My father and his mother and brother were devastated by the suicide. Furthermore, soon after, my grandmother began to have financial difficulty to run the household. The financial hardship necessitated drastic changes in their lifestyle.

At the time of my grandfather's suicide my father was only six years old and greatly needed fatherly guidance in planning his education. Fortunately this was provided by his uncles who were all high-ranking military officers as generals. They took over the education of my father and enrolled him in the military academy. In late 19th Century the military academy was run by Russian generals appointed by the Czar of Russia. It was the policy of the academy to accept the boys of noble families for training from the age of elementary school until they became officers in the Persian army. As a result my father became very fluent in the Russian language and developed friendship with the officers of the Imperial Russian army and an interest in their culture.

In the 19th Century, during the rule of Ghajar kings, the top super powers, Russia and England, had divided Iran into two regions of political influence, England in the south and Russia in the north. The major political influence of Russia centered on controlling the Persian army. The most prominent unit of the Persian army was the Cossack Brigade, which was an elite Cavalry unit formed in 1879. The unit was modeled after the Caucasian Cossack regiments of the Imperial Russian Army, wearing a Russian-style uniform. Until 1917 Russian officers, who were also employed in the Russian army, commanded the Persian brigade.

Upon the graduation from the military academy, my father joined the Persian Cossack brigade as an officer. He was a dashing officer, a very good-looking young man, and a great equestrian. His experiences in the brigade have been detailed in a recently published book (5) several decades after his death. The book

My father as an officer in the Persian Cossack brigade

is based on a serialized memoir published in a leading Persian weekly magazine over 40 years ago. The book provides eye witness accounts of the great efforts of the Persian Cossack brigade to save Iran from being torn apart by the uprising of native tribes and the invasions of foreign powers during the end of the 19th and the beginning of the 20th century. In the book he provides extensive information on the names, actions, and sacrifices of the Persian military commanders who participated in the above great efforts. My father showed incredible bravery as an officer fighting many battles in Iran. In these battles he came very close to being killed on several occasions. These battles are detailed in his book entitled *Thirty Years with Reza Shah, written* in Farsi. As described in the previous chapter, Reza Shah was the founder of the Pahlavi Dynasty.

The most serious threat to the integrity of Iran as a country occurred during the invasion of the Bolsheviks. My father, as one of the military commanders, was sent to fight them.

Unfortunately, he was captured by the Bolsheviks and put in jail. He believed that the Russians were going to execute him. To save himself from execution, he came up with a clever idea. He wrote to the Bolshevik commander that he has been trained since childhood by the officers of the Russian army and now he is eager to join the Red Army. He thought that if he could get the Russians to trust him, he might have a chance of escaping.

The Bolshevik commander summoned him to his office to tell him he is willing to enroll him in the Red Army and his first mission will be to go to Russia with a group of army officers to bring back the needed military supplies. After he established trusting relations with his Russian comrades, he began to think of a plan to escape. He thought he could take a chance on joining a group of Torkamans, who regularly went to the Caspian Sea to fish on a sailboat. He bribed their boss to take him along as a fisherman on their next trip, but to let him off on an Iranian Caspian Sea shore. My father dressed up as a Torkaman fisherman and spent several anxious days on the sea until they reached a safe port on the Caspian shore. His return to Tehran was a great joy for the family, especially for my mother, because they all believed he had been executed by the Bolsheviks.

A memorable experience of my father's in the Cossack brigade was his friendship with Reza Khan. As discussed in a previous chapter, he was a rising star of the brigade and became king as the founder of Pahlavi dynasty. They fought together many battles to defend the country. In 1925 my father and a group of Cossack officers took over the capital of Iran to overthrow the corrupt and incompetent Ghajar dynasty and to establish Reza Khan as the king. The memoir of my father, *30 Years with Reza Shah in the Army*, has been published (5).

It is not clear why he ended his military career at the relatively young age of 45. It appears that he did not play politics with his superiors. Despite his great military achievements (See his memoir.) and over 30 years of flawless military service to the nation, his promotion to higher ranks was denied. It is also not clear why my father did not use his acquaintance with the Reza Shah and his uncle who was the highest military officer in the Reza Shah army (Marshal Yazdan Panah) to overcome his difficulties with his immediate superiors to advance to the rank of general, like his father and uncles.. When he retired from the army, he supplemented his military pension with the income from investments in real estate. Therefore, we were able to remain as an upper class family in Tehran.

In early 20th century Europeans societies began to enjoy American inventions like car, telephone, phonograph, radio, etc. My father was among the first Iranians who acquired the above inventions. He was so ahead of his time when he obtained his radio. There was not as yet any radio station in Iran or surrounding countries. The only station that he could get on his radio was from Egypt. We therefore every evening listened to music broadcast from Cairo. I remember my father became fond of listening to singing of a famous Egyptian woman by the name of Omi Corsum. When Tehran finally built a radio station, I became an avid listener of their literary declamations and classical music.

I am certain that my ancestors both on mother and father sides for a long time played great roles in shaping the Iranian history. Unfortunately for the following reasons I am unable to give much detail. First, except for my father, no one wrote a book on his or her memories. This was not customary in the Moslem culture. Family history was passed along verbally. Second, my mother died when I was too young to ask her about my ancestors. When I left Iran I was a teenager and too busy with the challenges of growing up to have time to probe my father for the ancestral history. He died 12 years after I left Iran before I could return to see him. Third, I recently discovered that I have lost my command of my native tongue, namely Persian. The origins of the Persian language is Indo-European, and highly different from Arab or Indian languages. The above discovery came about when I decided to read the book of poetry of my grandfather and the recently published memoirs of my father. This even extended to my attempts to read my own poetry and short stories written when I was a teenager. It seems that I paid a great price for never reading any book written in Persian or hardly talking to anyone in Farsi for the many (over 64) years that I have lived in America. Now I remember that my grandfather warned me of this possibility when I was reading his poetry as a child. Apparently, he had met some Iranian students who had gone to Europe for their university educations who had difficulty speaking Farsi when they returned. One of my great regrets of losing reading Farsi is that I can no longer enjoy reading Persian poetry. It is over 1,000 years accumulation of art treasures. There is nothing like it in any other culture. The poets had to be masters of selecting words that matched because when you read Persian poetry it should have a rhythm to sound like you are singing.

The most famous Persian poets lived between the 10th and the 14th centuries. In the West, the most well-known Persian poets are Omar Khayyam and Rumi, but there are others. For example, there is the 10th century poet Ferdowsi whose poetry revived the pre-Islamic Persian civilization and language. My name, Siamak, and those of my siblings came from his monumental book of poetry called *Shahnameh* or *The Book of Kings*. Siamak was a king who like King Arthur was a brave and benevolent king. When I was a teenager in Iran and writing and reading Persian poetry, my favorite poet was Hafez who lived in the 14th century. Like other people I would consult him when I was sad because he would have cheerful advice.

4   My Mother and Her Ancestors

My mother's ancestors were Persian gentlemen farmers because they owned large properties in an area called Tafresh, which is located in the center of the country. In the middle of the 19th Century, there was severe drought for several years, impairing farming and resulting in economic hardship. My great grandfather Kazem Khan was forced to abandon farming and move to Tehran to enter into a new business. He was a very literate man with a great knowledge of the Persian language. At the time of the arrival of Kazem Khan to Tehran, there was a large population of illiterates. He therefore opened an office to help these peoples with writing and reading their letters and preparing their various documents.

He did such a great job that his business grew and he became famous. The Ghajar King (Naser Din Shah) heard about him and became interested in meeting him and therefore he was summoned to the Royal Court. After several meetings, the king became so

impressed with my great grandfather's talents and honesty that
he appointed him to become the royal treasurer. From the income
of his business and the salary from the king, he became quite a
wealthy man and founder of the Kazemi family.

Quite uncommon in Iran, Kazem Khan used his wealth to
become a big philanthropist. He bought a block of buildings to
become the low-rent housing for the poor. He built a mosque
for praying, preaching, educating, and feeding the poor. Lastly,
he endowed income for covering the expenses of the above
organizations by forming a foundation. The Kazemi Mosque still
stands in southern Tehran and is fully in use. The most senior
member of my mother's family (the Kazemis) is responsible for
running the foundation and the mosque.

The government has taken over the beautiful mansion of Kazem
Khan, which is located near the mosque and has turned it into a
museum. I have heard recently that a book has been published
about my great grandfather's (Kazem Khan) mansion and mosque.
The book is written in Farsi and is entitled *Saray-e Kazemi*. The

Kazemi mosque

The pool to wash your hands
and face before praying in the
Kazemi mosque

publisher is Ghlomreza Sahab.

When I visited the mosque, my cousin Javad Kazemi, was in charge of the Mosque and the Foundation. Behind him are the pictures of some of the previous Kazemis who served in the above role.

My mother's family and relatives are descendants of Kazem Khan and, therefore, are called Kazemi. My mother's father was a minister in the Royal Court of Ghajar. His given title from the king was "Vazir Davab" meaning the minister of transportation.

My mother, called Nezhat, was the darling of the family because she was the last child to be born and the only girl after the birth of six boys. She was nursed by a highly experienced and loving nanny and tutored at home. All these attentions did not spoil her because she grew up to be a woman of most gentle manners and kind disposition. She hardly got angry or had an unkind word for anybody. In short, she was a combination of saint and angel. Her unexpected death (to be described in the next chapter), when she was only in her 40s, was the most painful and life-changing experience of my childhood. My mother was such a gentle lady

Meeting my cousin Javad Kazemi in his office in the Kazemi Mosque. He was the most senior family member and therefore, in charge of the Mosque. The pictures behind him are the previous heads of the family.

that I never saw her get angry or argue with anyone.

In contrast, my father had an entirely different temperament. He was brought up in a military school since age of 7 or 8 and when graduated he became a military officer until he retired.

Consequently, he had gotten used to issuing orders and when they had not been properly followed he would blow his temper. On occasions, my mother could not tolerate my father and would leave our house to go to stay with her oldest brother who was like a father to her. I was a kid then and could not tell what the problem was. All I remember is that shortly after her departure my father would go to my uncle's house to beg her to come back. In the next chapter, I will discuss the radical changes in my father after my mother's sudden death.

My mother's picture, probably taken in the early 1930's. My mother was one of the first women to abandon the Islamic dress code of hijab (wearing chador) as had been ordered by the ayatollahs.

5 Growing Up in Tehran

Childhood Period

As I have already mentioned, when I was born as the first son I was treated like a crown prince. See my picture when I was a toddler. I was given much attention and brought up with great care. As a result I became a demanding boy that one could call a little spoiled. My wishes were commonly honored. For example, I developed great attachment to my mother and amazingly I still remember that I would not let go of breast feeding until I was too old for it. She had to use all sorts of maneuvers to wean me off.

Another remarkable recollection of childhood is that when I was around 4 years old, I decided I would like to become a photographer. Unfortunately in 1930s, the camera operation was complicated and therefore when my parents bought me a camera I realized I had gone overboard in asking for things.

When I was a few years old, my family moved to different cities in Iran. This was because of my father's job as a military officer.

I am shown in a white shirt and my brother in a black shirt. My mother is sitting between us. My father is standing behind us in the center holding the cane. My two sisters are seated, one next to me and one next to my brother. The people around my father are members of his staff. At the time of this photograph Reza Shah had already abolished wearing the Russian uniform for military men and Islamic chadors for women.

He would be assigned to different cities as the military commander. Among the cities that I lived in, Shiraz, the capital of Fars, made the most lasting impression on me. As shown in the photo with my family, I look happy living in Shiraz, because I am smiling.

Not far away from Shiraz was Persepolis, the ancient capital of Achaemenes, the king who created the world's first superpower empire. My father took me there to show me the remains of the buildings that once were the most majestic buildings in the world, before they were burned in revenge by Alexander the Great. I think he is called great because he conquered the Persian Empire.

My formal education began when I was 6 years old. I was sent to a nearby kindergarten that was run by the head master of a girl's school. Elementary and high schools for boys and girls were separate, but mixing was permitted in the kindergarten. I remember enjoying the art work and grown up girls, such as my sisters, coming to my class to see the little kids.

This began my lifelong attraction to pretty women. Since I was also considered a "pretty boy," most of the women who came to visit my parents wanted to kiss me. I remember enjoying only the kisses from the women who were pretty and young. After kindergarten my parents enrolled me in an elementary school that was very close to our house. Since I was having such a good time at home I thought going to school would end having freedom to have fun. I was reluctant to go, but soon after I was persuaded to go I realized how wrong I was. Not knowing that I would grow to love going to school so much that I would remain in it as a university professor for life.

During the years that I was going to the elementary school I was always searching for ideas that would allow me to be like adults. For example, I opened a store in our house to sell goods to family and friends. I converted a storage room to look like a store with appropriate lights and store hours. The merchandise included a variety of things like newspapers, pencils, candy bars, old magazines, etc.

When I got older I became more sophisticated in my ambition to be innovative. For example, I became interested in becoming a moviemaker. The first thing I had to do was to have a home projector that was not yet available in Tehran during the 1930s. Therefore, I had to make one. I did this by putting together a wooden box, a series of magnifying glasses, and a powerful electric light. The second thing I had to do was to make my own film. I did this by buying old film from the cinemas. Then I erased the old pictures on the film and replaced it with my own drawings. For sound effects I provided my live narration. For audience I invited my family and relatives who came with enthusiasm. I never found out whether the enthusiasm was for seeing my movie or for the food and drinks that my parents provided afterwards. I suspect it was a combination of both.

When I was going to elementary school one day my father took me out of school to show me the military academy. The head of the school was a general who knew my father from the days when both were students in the military academy. My father's intention was to interest me in enrolling in the military academy because all my father's ancestors were military officers. When I learned of his intention, I ran out of the office of the headmaster protesting his intention, because my own intention was to become a writer. As a child one of my hobbies was to hide in our little library and write short stories without showing them to anyone. As I will mention this became my passion as I grew up.

My closest friend during childhood was my brother Hooshang. Since he was two years younger I used to boss him around. Although I also had two sisters by the names of Roshanak and Faranak, they were too much older to play with me. All our names were chosen by our father from the Persian epic historic poems of Ferdosi called the Shahnameh (Book of Kings). Ferdosi was born in the 10th Century. He is credited as the savior of the Farsi language from the Arab invaders and the keeper of glorious pre-Islamic Persian history. Before the Pahlavi kings it was common practice to use the Islamic Arabic names like Mohammad and Ali. My father did not have much interest in the Islamic Arab culture, but like his old friend Reza Shah, he was greatly interested in reviving the pre-Islamic Persian culture. Therefore, all our names came from the Ferdosi's *Shahnameh*. For example, he named me Siamak which was the name of a great mythical Persian king similar to King Arthur, who lived in the ancient time.

My childhood, by and large, was a happy period for me. I greatly loved my mother and greatly respected my father. Their close supervision of my activities did not bother me. In the wintertime when we lived in Tehran during the day I would go to school and during the weekend I would play with my brother and frequently go to a big lunch at one of my uncles' homes or they would come to our home. Our biggest meal of the day was always served at lunch.

My brother Hooshang, another ancient Persian name, and I looked forward to spending the evenings with our parents. We would sit around a covered table kept warm by burning coals under a table called "corsee." There were delicious snacks like fruits and hot baked potatoes and sweet red beets called "labu." My father would enjoy his vodka or red wine prepared for him by the Armenians who were renting his various houses. The rest of us would drink various juices. For evening entertainment, my mother would read aloud the Farsi translation of various French novels. My favorite book was *The Three Musketeers* written by Alexandre Dumas. I was so absorbed by these heroes that when I visited Paris as a teenager I went looking for them.

Teenage Period

I am standing in front of the entrance of the old main building of the Alborz High School.

My teenage period began with my taking full command of my life away from my parents.

The first decision I had to make was choosing a high school. I looked at several public high schools, but none of them impressed me. I finally chose a high school that was unique in all Iran. It was called Alborz College.

It was founded by the American missionaries. By the time I got there the missionaries had left Iran several years earlier. However, the school still had kept some of the Western influences like great sport facilities, dormitories, and a large campus. None of these could be found in any high school. The head of Alborz College had a doctorate in education from a European university and was a legend by the name of Dr. Modjtahedi. The school was located in northern boundary of Tehran, therefore with a great view of the Alborz Mountain. The surrounding neighborhood was recently developed in the Northern Tehran with the architecture following the modern European styles.

Academically, I put most of my effort to develop further my passion for writing short stories and poetry. My teachers, without exception, rated me as the best student in writing composition and always gave me the highest grade. In fact, commonly, my teachers asked me to read my short stories before the whole class. A great deal of my time at home was spent reading the

I was the founder and manager of a soccer team in Tehran.

novels of famous Western writers and the Persian poetry. Persian poets like Rumi, Omar Khayyam, and Hafez are the greatest in the world. The Persian poetry, when you read it in Farsi, sounds like a musical composition. The lyrical sound, created by the selection of matching words, is lost in translation. Because of my preoccupation with writing and literature, I was not doing well in my science courses, in fact commonly getting poor grades.

My second outburst of passion in the Alborz College was to develop great enthusiasm for playing sports like soccer and basketball. In fact this enthusiasm lead to my being asked to be co-manager of the first sport club in Tehran. The club was called

I was the founder and manager of a table tennis team
in Tehran that won the championship.

the bicyclist club in honor of its founder who was a champion bicyclist. Using this club, I founded soccer and ping pong teams to play in the city tournaments.

In addition to professional sports, I became interested in going hunting. A cousin invited me to go hunting with him at his parents' country estate in northern Tehran that resulted in a great accident. We were climbing a high hill in search of deer. He was coming behind me when suddenly I heard a gunshot and a loud scream. I

My picture while hunting.

turned around and ran down the hill to see what had happened. I
saw blood flowing from the right hand of my cousin. Apparently
he was using his loaded gun as a cane to climb the hill and the gun
discharged a bullet into his hand when he hit the gun against a hard
rock. The only thing I could do was to run as fast as I could to the
nearest village and ask for help. Fortunately I found a doctor who
was able to take him to a nearby hospital. He was lucky that after
many operations they were able to save his hand although not its
function. The incident terminated my interest in going hunting and
since then I have never touched any guns.

As I was enjoying life as a teenager, suddenly a great tragedy
hit me. One day late in the afternoon, I returned home from all
day being in my high school. I found our house full of people,
including many of my mother's relatives, all with a gloomy face.
They told me that in the morning after I left for my school, my
mother fell into a deep coma. I knew my mother was being treated
for high blood pressure by a family doctor, but I did not know how
she was being treated and whether high blood pressure was a threat
to her life. In the early 1940s there was no effective treatment for
hypertension, which probably caused a fatal stroke. I was totally
unprepared for this tragedy because that morning I had my usual

breakfast with my mother before I left for my high school. As a consequence I was devastated by coming to this tragedy that was so unexpected.

Soon after my arrival I rushed to her room to see her. I found my mother unconscious and being watched by one of my aunts. When my aunt saw me, she left the room and I became alone with my mother. It seemed that my mother had remained alive until I could say good-bye to her because shortly after I arrived she began to gasp. I was the only person in the room and did not know what to do. As a young boy I had never seen anybody dying or dead. So I knelt on the side of her bed and kept kissing her hand and crying. This was about 70 years ago, but the memory of that fateful night is still fully alive in my mind and each time that I think of it the grief comes back.

For a long time I refused to believe that this had happened. I greatly loved my mother and was very dependent on her. For example, one of my earliest concerns was who is going to cut my nails. The tragedy had an even greater effect on my younger brother , Hooshang, and father because my sisters and I had many outside interests, but my brother and father were totally dependent on my mother.

With the passing of my mother, our happy home became very quiet and depressed and dark. For example, my father became so quiet that he hardly talked to me. It became apparent to me that he greatly loved my mother and was lost without her. With my mother gone I was committed to take over planning of my life, although I was only an inexperienced teenager. I began to think a great deal about my future. After much thinking I came to the conclusion that I needed to pursue an occupation that would assure me of a steady high income to allow me to continue the life style that I had been used to. This led to my selection of the medical profession, which necessitated giving up my passion for becoming a novelist and a poet. It was to be only for a while because I thought that after I became a physician I could do both. My model for this was Anton Chekov, the greatest Russian playwright. However, as will be discussed in the next chapter, my medical life became so demanding that I had no time for pursuing my childhood ambition, namely to become a novelist.

After making this decision, the question became where I should go to get the best medical education possible. I consulted many experts of medical education and they all recommended Johns Hopkins University in America. When I told my father of my plan to go to America he became very upset with my going so far away from him, a distance of near half of the world. He insisted as a compromise I could go to Europe because it was much closer and my sister, Roshan, was in Paris studying fashion design in Sorbonne University. Another alternative was to go to Sweden because my cousin was Ambassador there. After arguing for several weeks that America was the best place for my medical education, he finally gave his consent.

In the 1950s KLM had the monopoly of air travel from Tehran to Europe and America. As a result the fare was very expensive. To reduce the cost I learned that I could charter a KLM plane. I knew a whole bunch of my classmates at the Alborz High School who were going to Europe to enter the universities. It occurred to me that I could charter a plane to share with these classmates. So I contacted KLM and they agreed to my chartering a plane. My friends wanted to know how they can pay me for their airline ticket. Since I was too young to have a bank account, I told them they can pay me in cash. I took a suitcase to collect the very large sum of Iranian money that they were bringing to me. It took several days to complete the collections.

During this time I was living in fear of something might happen to my suitcase. I was greatly relieved the day when I was able to take the suitcase to the officer of KLM in Tehran.

A few days before our departure, the government announced that there was a new policy on foreign exchange. This policy was brought about by England freezing all the Iranian assets in response to Iran nationalizing its oil. Because of the shortage of foreign money the government had ordered the banks not to exchange any Iranian money. Suddenly I was faced with a crisis because without this we could not go abroad. I gathered a select group of students, who wanted to go abroad for undergraduate or post-graduate studies, in my house for a meeting to discuss what to do. We decided we should have a peaceful sit down demonstration in the Parliament to protest the government decision. In the late afternoon when the deputies had gone home, we peacefully entered the Parliament, the Majlis, and took over the chamber of the deputies. We informed the officials why we were there and we spread our blankets to sleep during the night.

My group and I (the first one on the left) meeting with the King (standing in the center) in his private office.

We were awakened in the morning by the military aide of the king (Mohammad Reza Shah Pahlavi) to go to the royal palace to meet with him. I chose a few members of my group to go with me.

The King was very kind to us and agreed to our demand. He was supportive of our wanting to go abroad for our education, because he had done the same for himself. He immediately got on the phone with the prime minister and convinced him of the importance of us going abroad for education. The prime minister was Dr. Mossadegh, who was my greatly beloved hero. He was

My group and I (the first one on the right) are all looking happy leaving the King's palace. Please note that among my friends I was the most elegantly dressed person. This was because my clothing was prepared by my personal tailor.

going through a very difficult time fighting colonial England. This will be discussed more fully in the last chapter.

Therefore, the obstacle of currency exchange was removed and we headed to the airport for departure in the fall of 1950. All my immediate family came to the airport to see me off. When I was kissing my tearful father good-bye, I did not know that it would be the last time I would see him. For the first 12 years of my living in America, I did not dare go to Iran because of fear that I may get drafted into the military service and not be able to return to continue my education. During this long absence my father passed away.

The night before my leaving Tehran I insisted that we go to a photographer for a family picture. I am glad that I did this because it has kept the memory of my family alive. The only one missing in this picture is my second oldest sister, Roshan, who was away

My older sister (Faranak) is sitting between me and my father. My brother (Hooshang) is standing behind us. The two girls (Goli and Nari) are Faranak's daughters. The only family member missing in the picture is my sister Roshan, who was studying in the Sorbonne in Paris.

in Paris attending the Sorbonne University. As you can see in the family photograph everyone is smiling except my father who looks gloomy. I think he probably was thinking that this could be the last time he would see me. If this was his thought, it sadly turned out that he was right.

My two sisters became pioneers for women's liberation. Faranak became the first woman teacher in the University of Tehran. She then was appointed to become the Minister of Education and later to become the Cultural Attaché in the Iranian Embassy in Turkey. Roshan after returning from Paris became the first woman to establish a fashion studio in Tehran. Her clients included the members of the royal family. Both sisters were fluent in French and English and traveled frequently in Europe and America to attend meetings. My brother Hooshang studied pharmacology at the University of Pennsylvania and became the head of Pharmacology in one of the major hospitals in Tehran.

Part 2: Medical Education in America

6 Premedical Education at Johns Hopkins

Around 1950 when I was leaving Iran, the Tehran Airport was quite small and a very friendly place. There were no guards or security personnel and our plane was the only plane scheduled to fly when we were in the airport. As a result we had the airport to ourselves.

Our flight was in the early morning. Our family and friends had gotten up early to come to see me off. They were allowed to gather on the tarmac. When I ascended the stairs to enter the plane, I turned around to have a last look at my family. I saw them all wiping their eyes. I was too excited to cry. It was the first time I was going to experience flying and seeing the world. The plane was on the small side, because the big passenger jets had not yet been introduced. But this did not prevent my excited friends from initiating a singing and dancing party in the aisles of the plane when it took off. This scared the captain about the plane safety and several times came over to ask my friends to take their seats. Apparently, too much weight concentrated in one area of the plane was causing problems with keeping the plane's balance. Although the plane's destination was Paris, it had to land in Athens, Greece for fueling. Therefore, I got a chance to see Athens from the low-flying airplane. When we arrived in Paris, it was mid-afternoon. You gain time by flying from Tehran to Paris. My second older sister, Roshan, was waiting for me in the airport. She had been in Paris for several years to study fashion design in the Sorbonne University. Therefore, I was elated to see her.

I said good-bye to my friends who flew with me because no one was coming to America and each one was going to a different place in Europe.

My sister took me to the left bank of Paris where she had an apartment. She reserved a room for me in a hotel near her place. She took me to my hotel and told me to rest for a few hours to recover from my long journey and she would be back in the evening to take me out to dinner. I was too excited to be able to rest. Therefore, I decided to leave the hotel and look for my childhood heroes, the musketeers (see the last chapter). When I left my hotel it was around 5 o'clock in the afternoon. To my disappointment I did not see any musketeer. Instead, I saw the first example of social freedom in Paris, which I still vividly remember. There was a large crowd of people walking in the sidewalk in front of my hotel. On a bench in front of the hotel, there was a couple sitting in a very tight embrace and passionately kissing each other. This was my first experience of seeing lovemaking in public, but even more surprising was to see that no one even bothered to turn their head to look at this couple – something unimaginable in Tehran!

My main curiosity for sight-seeing in Paris was to see the Avenue des Champs-Élysées. When I was growing up in Tehran, my sisters commonly referred to Champs-Élysées as the center of fashion and elegance. Therefore, I asked my sister to take me there. It was the most beautiful boulevard I had ever seen. It was quite wide and lined with tall trees. There were many enticing cafes and shops. It began with a majestic square called Place de la Concorde and ended with the imposing Arc de Triomphe. However, I did not see anyone more fashionable or glamorous than those I used to see in the streets of the Northern Tehran.

To open my eyes to the sexual freedom in Paris, my sister bought tickets to take me to see the Folies Bergère. I did not like the show. In fact, I was bored. For my last day in Paris, my sister planned to give me a tour of her university. I was impressed with the Sorbonne, but I did not like to get caught between the fights of Communists and Nationalists. My sister said this happens quite often because Communists are fighting for power.

After Paris the KLM flew me to Amsterdam. As a reward for my work to arrange the charter flight from Tehran to Paris, the company wanted to treat me to an all paid weekend in Holland. I arrived at night and a chauffeur and a hostess were waiting for me in the airport. They took me to my hotel and I immediately went to bed because I was so tired. I had a good night's sleep and when I work up in the morning I saw Amsterdam from my beautiful hotel room. I was greatly charmed by the beauty of the city. My hotel was located on a river bank. The most astonishing view was to see no car passing in front of my hotel, but instead I saw huge traffic of bicycles going in both directions. I had never seen this before.

It seemed that the traffic lights were for the bicycles. I had a grand weekend in Amsterdam and promised myself to come back when I could. On my subsequent visit I was disappointed to see that the cars had replaced bicycles as the source of traffic in the streets of Amsterdam.

After the weekend the KLM flew me to Nuremberg, Germany to pick up more passengers. Again like Athens the low-flying airplane allowed me to see Nuremberg from the air. I was struck with the hard-working Germans rebuilding the city from the destruction it had suffered during World War II. I was impressed with seeing the German women working together with the men in rebuilding the airport. I had never seen women as construction workers before. This was probably unique to the period of German recovery from the war destructions.

My KLM flight from Germany to the American continent was smooth. After 18 hours of flight, our plane needed refueling when it reached Newfoundland, Canada. Although it was only October, I was surprised to see so much snow on the ground. From Newfoundland we flew to Washington, DC. When I got off the plane, for the first time in my life I felt deeply alone in a new world. There was not any family member around to guide me. Not speaking English became a challenge to find my way in Washington. I tried to take advantage of a few English words that I had learned in high school. Applying this limited knowledge I was able to find a hotel in Washington. When I got to my hotel, a black man took my suitcase to carry it to my room. I had never seen a black man when I was growing up in Tehran. My nurse had taken advantage of this to use it as a scare tactic to control me. She would say, "If you do not behave an African will come and eat you." This fear had been imbedded so deeply in my psyche that it kept me awake all night. Happily, afterwards I was able to get rid of this fear and become very close friends with many African-American students.

The next morning, after a good night's sleep, I picked up my suit case and checked out of my hotel and took a train to Baltimore. When I reached Baltimore, in the train station I told a taxi driver to take me to Johns Hopkins University.

Before coming to America, I asked several medical doctors who had studied in Europe which is the best medical school in America. They all said Johns Hopkins in Baltimore.

Therefore, it was natural that for my first attempt to enter a medical school I would go there to present myself. After I was let off the taxi, I went directly to the Dean's office. I told the secretary that I have travelled all the way from Persia to see the dean. In those days nobody knew Iran, but most people knew Persia. She was so impressed she immediately ushered me in even without any appointment. The dean warmly greeted me. I put down my suitcase and said I have come from Persia with the single purpose of studying medicine at your university. He seemed speechless. He had never seen a Persian and even more unusual, a gutsy young man who, without going through the process of applying for admission, wanted to enter the medical school without even being fluent in English. He seemed impressed with my courage and determination and became greatly interested in wanting to have a Persian student in his university. He told me that he would take me into his premedical program after I become proficient in the English language. In Iran and Europe people enter medical school after finishing high school, but I did not know that this was not the

Waiting to entertain a date in the reception hall of my dormitory at Johns Hopkins

61

case in America. One has to complete premedical education before being considered for admission to the medical school. He advised me to take a semester in the neighboring university, namely the University of Maryland, to learn English, and not to be afraid of failing my courses. He told me to come back after I finished the semester. He seemed confident that by then I would be ready to become a premedical student at the Johns Hopkins. In fact, he said he could arrange for my admission to the University of Maryland. I told him to go ahead and he immediately got on the phone. In retrospect, in face of the rarity of a Persian student in America, I could have gone to any university, but I decided to stay with my original plan, namely, to study medicine at Johns Hopkins. Therefore, I took a taxi from Johns Hopkins University to the University of Maryland, which was about 40 minutes away. They were waiting for me when I got there. They assigned me a room in the dormitory and a faculty adviser to plan my courses. So I began my life in America.

Besides language, I had a great deal to learn about American culture and customs and way of life. For the first time in my life there was no servant around to prepare food for me. For example, I was a very skinny boy and used to have snacks between meals. One of my favorite snacks was boiled egg. I had seen our servants how they prepared boiled eggs. They put them around samovar (used for making tea) and let the steam coming from the samovar to cook the eggs. Therefore, I thought I could prepare boiled eggs in my room in the dormitory. I bought a dozen eggs and put them all in the bathroom sink and let the hot water to run over them for 30 minutes. I was greatly disappointed that the experiment failed, since when I cracked each egg it was completely raw. So my first attempt showed me that I need to learn a lot about cooking.

Since the fall semester had already begun, I had to wait until the spring semester to take courses. Meanwhile, my faculty advisor assigned me to a graduate student in the language department to work with me to improve my knowledge of the English language.

Initially, when I wanted to speak with people I tried to translate Persian words to English. This commonly caused laughter. For example, in Persian the word for "falling down" is "eating the ground." When I said this to my friends to explain my accident, they said, "How could you eat the ground?" From things like this I learned that when I want to talk to my friends, I should not think of Persian words, but to think of English words.

The University of Maryland is located in a small town called College Park, which is close to Washington, DC, about 20 minutes by train. Therefore, often on the weekend I would go to Washington to socialize with a few Iranian friends who lived there. Among these there were two important men: one was the cultural attaché and the other the military attaché in the Iranian Embassy.

The cultural attaché, who was the uncle of the king, was responsible for all of the Iranian students in America. He seemed to like me and wanted to be kept informed of my progress.

The military attaché was the uncle of my closest friend in Tehran and I was asked to look him up. I greatly enjoyed meeting him and his family. I would often get an invitation for the Sunday dinners to be with his family. They had only one daughter who was very beautiful and charming and knew Washington well and so became my guide. My feeling for her grew to become a serious love. I lost control of myself and proposed marriage. Her mother saved me from destroying my plans for my future. The mother took me to their library and said privately, "we like you a lot, but you are too young to marry our daughter. You have so many challenges ahead of you to reach your goal of becoming a doctor that for a long time you will not have time to take care of a family." Her advice was so powerful to me that I gave up the idea of marriage. As it turned out, she was absolutely right and she saved me from making a serious mistake. Looking back, I realized my irrational marriage proposal was prompted by my pain of being lonely and far away from home, which I thought I could treat by establishing a family in America. As I will discuss, I became so absorbed in my studies that I completely forgot that I was lonely.

After this I greatly reduced my social visits in Washington and replaced it with visiting many monuments and historic places in Washington. The places I liked most were the Lincoln Memorial and the White House. The Lincoln Memorial has a simple, but very elegant design. You can almost feel his commanding presence.

In my studies of human histories, two leaders have my greatest respect and admiration. One is Abraham Lincoln and the other is Cyrus the Great, a Persian king who lived over 2,500 years ago (see Chapter 2). Lincoln freed blacks from slavery in America and Cyrus freed the Jews from slavery in Babylon.

Both spoke most eloquently in defense of human rights. My attraction to the White House was prompted by seeing that the most powerful leader in the world lived in a simple mansion that in 1950 was open to the public. You could walk around it and through the fence see the garden. It had none of the grandiosity of royal palaces in Europe like Buckingham and Versailles.

The semester at the University of Maryland went smoothly. As was predicted by the Dean of Johns Hopkins University, I failed all my courses, but became fluent in English. Therefore, I went back and the Dean seemed happy to see me. I was immediately enrolled for the summer semester. So began my years at Hopkins. Unlike the University of Maryland, I found the Hopkins campus beautifully designed and attractive. All buildings had the classic look of an old campus. The library and the dormitory buildings were quite elegantly furnished. I was given a plush room that had no comparison to my room in the University of Maryland. My roommate who became my first American friend was a Jewish fellow, Gene Galen, from outside of New York City. He was very smart and quite a friendly person. Like me he was also a "premed." Therefore, we had much in common to become close friends.

Like most of the people he did not know much about Persia, but was very interested to learn from me. My other close friend was a black graduate student who was very charming and intelligent. Although he was not a "premed" we had common interests in art and literature. One day I suggested we leave the campus and go to town for dinner. He told me Baltimore is a segregated town and blacks are not admitted to restaurants that served the whites. I was absolutely shocked to hear this because I had not known any segregation when I was growing up in Tehran. I could not believe that a culturally advanced country like America would have such an uncivilized custom.

The subsequent schools that I attended, like Jefferson Medical

College, Harvard, and MIT, did not have the impact that Hopkins had on me. I went through a great metamorphosis.

I changed from a passionate writer of fiction to a very serious basic scientist. When I was in Alborz College in Tehran, I hated my science courses, but in Hopkins I loved every science course that I took. This included a series of courses in mathematics, chemistry, biology, atomic physics, and biochemistry. I did very well in each course. My grade were either "A" or "H" (honor). I became so absorbed in basic science that I began to think of abandoning my plan to become a medical doctor, but go for a doctorate in biophysics. But the reality assessment of my future convinced me that if I go back to Iran I will not be able to find any job as a biophysicist, but I will have many opportunities as a medical doctor. Therefore, I gave up the idea.

I was very happy with my life as a student at Hopkins, that except for an occasional date, I hardly left the campus. Truly I was inspired by my courses and professors. The only person that I did not like was the Chief of Administration. She was frequently pressuring me for payments on my tuition and dormitory expenses. In early 1950s it was very hard to communicate with my father in Iran. Making a telephone call was not easy and letters took a long time to reach there. Johns Hopkins was a very expensive university. This was also a huge financial burden on my father because he had to pay a great deal of Persian money for each dollar he purchased from the bank. Sending money overseas required going through a series of procedures. This periodically resulted in a long delay in my getting money from Iran. The administrator did not care about my problems and wanted me to pay on time. There were times that I was alone and penniless and did not know when I was going to get my financial allowance. But I did not let this occasional poverty to distract me from my studies. I always knew that my father would come through with my need for money. To reduce the burden on my father I tried to finish my premedical education in three years instead of four years. I succeeded in this goal by taking a heavy load of courses each semester and taking credits for several courses, like history, philosophy, art appreciation, by taking their final exams. I was well-versed in these courses because of my prior high school education in the Alborz High School in Tehran.

My biggest anxiety during my premedical education was whether I would get into a medical school when I was finished. The reason for this anxiety was that in 1950s there were not as many medical schools in the country as there are today. There was also stiff competition for getting into a medical school. The reason for this was in the 1950s there were many veterans with the G.I. bill. The best use of G.I. Bill was to get a free medical education.

Therefore, they were mostly applying to get into medical schools. I sought the advice of my faculty advisor. I told him I do not wish to stay in Baltimore because I had come to dislike it greatly. In 1950s Baltimore was an ugly city and did not have much to offer. There were mostly bars and red-light districts in downtown, and not very safe to walk there at night.

Furthermore, as a southern city, there was intense prejudice against blacks. The upper class Baltimoreans lived in their beautiful houses in the suburbs and for recreation they went to their country clubs, for activities like golf, horseback riding, or hunting. In a recent visit to Baltimore, I was amazed to see how dramatically the city has changed since my days when I was living there. It has become a beautiful harbor city with many cultural and recreational facilities with the disappearance of prejudice against blacks.

When I told my advisor I did not wish to stay in Baltimore, he asked where I would like to move. I told him I would like to move away from the south and go north to cities like Philadelphia or New York. He suggested that for Philadelphia I should apply to the Jefferson Medical College, which is one of the oldest medical schools in the country, and in New York, I should apply to Columbia, which has the best reputation in that city. Although I did not know much about these schools, I followed his suggestion and applied to the two medical schools. After two weeks, unexpectedly, I received a letter of acceptance from the Jefferson Medical College. All of my classmates at Hopkins were surprised with the speed of response to my application, especially in view of the fact that I had not yet taken the medical school entrance examination and had not been subjected to any interview. The reasons for such a quick response probably included the fact that my Hopkins professors wrote very strong letters of recommendation, my outstanding grades, and being a foreign student from Persia, which they had never heard of. The Admission Committee probably considered me valuable and wanted to grab me before others had a chance to consider me. Sure enough about a month later I received a letter of invitation from the Columbia Medical School. Unfortunately, by then I had accepted the offer from Jefferson and had paid them the required advanced payment on my expensive tuition, something I could not afford to lose. In retrospect, I should have gone to Columbia rather than Jefferson. Later I learned that Jefferson was an excellent school for people who wanted to enter the clinical practice of medicine, but I was interested in an academic career that allowed me to pursue both aspects of medicine: practice and basic research. This would have been possible at Columbia, but not easily at Jefferson.

After graduation, I left the Johns Hopkins with sadness because I had loved all my studies there. They had done something for me that I did not know I could do. They turned me from a passionate fiction writer to a hard-core passionate scientist. There was sadness when I packed all my stuff in an old car that I had bought the week before. There was also fear that without much practice of driving my first car, and without a driver's license, I may get into trouble driving from Baltimore to Philadelphia. To my great delight I had a smooth ride and found lodging in one of the Jefferson Medical fraternity houses for the summer. The students were away for the summer. Therefore, except for the housekeeper, the house was empty of students. Early arrival gave me an opportunity to become familiar with the "City of Brotherly Love" (Philadelphia) and its many offerings. Then I took a month to go to New York City to visit my friends who lived there. Also I became familiar with the New York City that I had heard so much about.

7 Medical Education at Jefferson

There was no doctoral training as expensive as medical. Except for war veterans, scholarships for going to medical school were unheard of. Therefore, I began to worry about how my father was going to afford to send me large sums of money for my tuition and living expenses. I knew his main income was from his retirement fund, which was to provide enough support for him during his old days. Once again in my life I became extremely lucky. The cultural attaché in the Iranian Embassy was so impressed with my accomplishments at Johns Hopkins that he was compelled to report this to his Majesty the King. In fact, he reported that I was the best Iranian student in America. Apparently, the King was pleased to get this report. He promptly summoned my father to the Royal Palace to ask him what would be the best award he could bestow on me. My father replied financial support for me to be able to complete my medical education in America. The King granted me this award by ordering his personal foundation to carry out his wishes to cover my necessary expenses for the duration. I was so elated at the news that I stopped worrying about the money problems and totally concentrated on my courses.

Apparently, the King had become a fan of my father by reading his memoirs serialized in the most widely read weekly journal in Iran. A topic that was of great interest to the King was my father's memories of the King's father, Reza Khan, the founder of the Pahlavi dynasty. Before Reza Khan became king, he and my father were good friends in the Persian Cossack army and shared battle experiences in defending the country. As already mentioned, my father's memoirs have recently been published as a book (5).

The orientation procedures held at the medical college building were impressive. The lecture halls were rather large and furnished with antique furniture showing the old age of the college. The walls were decorated with the portraits of famous Jeffersonian doctors of the 19th Century. Among these was the famous Gross clinic showing Dr. Gross in his street clothes operating on a patient in the pit of a big amphitheater while medical students were watching. This painting by the great American painter, Thomas Eakins, is considered one of the greatest shows of American art and recently has been relocated to the Philadelphia Museum of Fine Arts for safekeeping.

The first year was mostly studying anatomy and histology.

Anatomy involved dissecting a cadaver. In the first day I was fearful to enter the dissecting hall. This was caused by remembering what happened to my cousin when he went to start dissecting his cadaver at the University of Tehran Medical School. When he lifted the cover of his cadaver, he saw it was his old nanny. He immediately fainted. When he was revived he left the room and never returned to the medical school. Fortunately, my cadaver turned out to be someone I had never met, but my partner and I gave him a name.

Studying anatomy and histology were all memorization exercises and turned out to be boring for me. This was a sharp contrast to my premedical studies that were mostly intellectual, requiring me to use my brain to figure out. After the first year there was increasing improvement in my liking of the medical school courses like biochemistry and physiology.

However, there were still courses like microbiology that were called "cookbook" by the students. In fact, lack of interest led me to fail the microbiology course. I was called into the dean's office to be lectured about my lack of enthusiasm and a threat of expulsion if I did not shape up.

I was also turned off by the quality of students at the Jefferson Medical School. They mostly seemed had been specifically prepared for a career in medicine without much exposure to history and literature. For example, they thought everyone from the Middle East was an Arab. Persians, including myself, consider it an insult to be called an Arab. Because for thousands of years Persia had an advanced civilization and Arabs remained mostly as barbarians until close to the 10th C C.E. when they became civilized. In fact, the nomadic Arabs who conquered Persia in the 7th C C.E. learned to become cultured from the Persians.

One day at a gathering of my classmates, I was asked what does your father do in your country? I replied that my father lives in a country that used to be called Persia and he is a "used camel dealer." This resulted in a great laughter and the cessation of calling me an Arab.

To improve my liking of going to medical school, I asked one of my most distinguished professors if I could work in his research laboratories. He was Dr. Karl Paschkis, a professor of medicine and head of endocrinology. His textbook of endocrinology was used in many medical schools for teaching. He was also well known for his research contributions. He seemed pleased to take me as a member of his research team. I was given a laboratory space and a research project of "endocrine regulation of the liver regeneration." I was turned on by my research project and any free time I had from attending my classes I used to work in my lab. This included every weekend and holiday. Among my peers, I was the only person who succeeded to publish two research papers in medical journals while still a medical student.

This brought me considerable fame as evidenced by my election as the president of the Jefferson Physiological Society and the Jefferson Research Society. My main job as president was to organize lectures and research seminars by distinguished guest speakers.

My biggest honor at Jefferson was receiving the Jefferson Gold Medal of Surgery on my graduation, which was held in the elegant Philadelphia Academy of Music in the presence of the popular governor of Pennsylvania, David Lawrence. The Gold Medal was in recognition of my contribution to the art and science of partial hepatectomy in experimental animals. I was deeply touched when the governor stepped forward to congratulate me.

8 Post-Medical Education at Harvard and MIT

After graduation I spent one additional year at Jefferson Medical College Hospital to do my internship. This was required for taking the state board exam for getting my medical license.

After five years in Philadelphia I came to the conclusion that I had had enough of Philadelphia and Jefferson Medical College and it was time to move on to a new place. I consulted my mentor, Dr. Paschkis. He strongly suggested that I should apply for my training in internal medicine to a Harvard hospital in Boston. He said he is a good friend of Dr. George Thorn, the chief of Medicine at one of these Harvard hospitals called Peter Bent Brigham, and he would be willing to write to him about me. The reason for their friendship was that both were endocrinologists. I was excited when I was accepted to the post medical training at Harvard.

When I got to Boston, I was overwhelmed with seeing so many famous hospitals like Peter Bent Brigham, Children, New England Deaconess, and Beth Israel surrounding the Harvard Medical School. They were all connected through the Longwood Avenue. In fact, I found a nice apartment on the Longwood Avenue, a block away from the medical school, for my residence to be very close to the Mecca of Medicine.

Not far from the Harvard hospitals there were many colleges and universities. Therefore, the area was full of students of all kinds, making me feel I am in an exciting academic and social paradise. To take advantage of having so many intellectual, professional, and social friends, I formed Bostoniensis Camerata. This was to emulate the Florentine Camerata, which was founded by Count Giovanni Bardi in Florence in the 16th Century. He would invite intellectuals, mostly people like composers and musicians, to perform original works at his house for discussion. This resulted in the creation of many masterpieces, like the first opera. I would create a romantic ambiance in my apartment, such as providing candle light and wine to get my guests in the mood. My dates for these events came largely from the Wellesley College and the Radcliffe College of Harvard. I understand recently there has been the formation of a musical group in Boston calling themselves Bostoniensis Camerata.

After I finished my residency in internal medicine, I applied to Dr. Seymour Gray, who was the chief of gastroenterology at the Peter Bent Brigham Hospital. He immediately accepted me. Shortly after I joined his program at Harvard he accepted a visiting professorship in the department of nutrition at Massachusetts Institute of Technology (MIT). The purpose was for Dr. Gray to move to MIT to help Dr. Nevin Scrimshaw, the chairman of the department of nutrition, to develop a clinical research center on the MIT campus. I was persuaded to sign up for a fellowship in the department of nutrition and work toward a PhD degree in the nutritional sciences. I could do all this without giving up my appointment at the Peter Bent Brigham Hospital, a principal teaching hospital at Harvard Medical School. I used this hospital to take care of GI patients and teach myself clinical gastroenterology.

In the early 1960s there was no teaching of clinical nutrition in any medical school and, consequently, except for a rare physician, almost all were ignorant of treating the nutritional problems of their patients. As a person searching for new frontiers in medicine, I thought I could use my MIT education to introduce clinical nutrition to the teaching and practice of medicine.

With the consent of Drs. Scrimshaw (Chairman of the Department of Nutrition) and Gray, I developed two research projects. The first was to study the intestinal absorption of amino acids (protein constituents) in the intestine of human volunteers. The techniques involved passing a multi-lumen tube to the small intestine and infusing through the tube solutions of amino acids. These studies, which were the first to examine the pattern of amino acid absorption in the small intestine of human subjects, revealed a highly selective pattern. The pattern ranged from fast to slow absorption.

My second study involved the treatment of obesity. So far back as my days in MIT, it was well known that the largest nutritional problem in America is obesity. Despite this knowledge there was very little attempt by practicing doctors to treat obesity. I thought there was a desperate need for someone to come out with a treatment plan and I thought that "the someone" was to be me.

Since the approved goal of MIT clinical research center was research and not patient care, my research protocol submitted for approval stated that I planned to study the effect of starvation on amino acid metabolism using obese subjects. My undeclared plan was to see whether by starvation I could bring the body weight to near normal. I admitted several highly enthusiastic subjects to the clinical research center. They were enthusiastic because I was planning to help them to lose weight with all the expenses covered by research grants from the National Institutes of Health (NIH). I totally starved them for two weeks. They were given only clear liquids and they lost between twenty to twenty-five pounds. On discharge from the clinical research center, I gave them instructions for a low-calorie diet at home and to come back to see me after a month. I was greatly disappointed that when they came back to see me. Almost every one of them had regained the lost weight. The experiment was not a total loss because I succeeded in making novel discoveries on the effect of starvation on amino acid metabolism. As I will discuss later, I did not give up trying to find a solution to treat obesity.

Part 3: Becoming Established in America

9 Return to Iran or Stay in America

In the early 1960s, when I was getting close to finishing my medical training, I began to think about my future. The central question was whether I should return to Iran or permanently stay in America. Because of all the financial support I had received from the King's foundation, I felt I had an obligation to go back and find out whether I could establish a career in academic medicine in Iran, by directly asking the King. I had not been back since I left Iran in 1950. I was also very curious to see what had happened to the country in the past 12 years. As I mentioned earlier, the reason for my not returning earlier was the fear of being drafted into military service. Now, I was beyond the drafting age.

Harvard used to have a charter flight to Europe in the summer for the students and faculty. I took advantage of this flight because the fare was inexpensive, but the flight from London to Tehran was by commercial plane and that the fare was expensive.

When I arrived in Tehran airport my family and friends were waiting for me. The only family member missing was my father who had died a couple of years earlier.

I was amazed with the growth of Tehran in the twelve years that I was away. It appeared to me that Tehran had changed from a Persian city to an American city. There was a large population of Americans living in Tehran. They were either working for the large American Embassy or representing many American companies. The popular hotels were Hilton and the Sheraton and the popular restaurants were the ones that were serving American fast food.

My sisters became busy trying to find an attractive and educated Persian girl from the famous families for me to consider for marriage. Unfortunately, I had already met the daughter of the American Consul in Tehran and had become attracted to her. She was a beautiful and intelligent girl who had come to Tehran to spend her summer vacation with her parents. She was a senior in an American university.

The only trip I took while in Iran was to go to the Caspian Sea where my brother-in-law, General Hamedi, was the commander of the army. He put a car and a driver at my disposal that allowed me to explore the beautiful coast of the Caspian Sea. I greatly enjoyed staying in the luxurious Ramsar Hotel overlooking the Caspian Sea. In the evening the hotel had an excellent romantic program of music and dancing under the stars. Champaign was served during the dancing.

I had to cut short my great trip to the Caspian and return to Tehran to try to get an appointment with the King to find out whether I had a future in Iran. I called the king's secretary and was told that the king is out of the country, but I could talk to the Minister of the Court. I accepted the invitation and was driven to the royal palace. I found the minister a very elegant and polite man who greeted me warmly. He was sorry the king was out of the country for he would have liked to have seen me. When I asked him about a career in academic medicine where I could combine basic research and clinical medicine, he seemed sad to tell me that as yet they have not set up laboratories for basic medical research at the university. He was, however, hopeful that they would have it in the future. As I will discuss, that happened nearly two decades later (Chapter 12). When I got up to leave, he asked me whether I could help his son to get into a medical school in America. The only answer I could give him was that I would be happy to talk to him when I get back to America.

When I returned from the royal palace, I told my sisters to stop searching for a Persian wife because I am returning to live permanently in the United States. In that case an American wife would be much better for me than a Persian wife.

On my return from Tehran to Boston, I planned to visit a few cities that were of great interest to me. These included: Istanbul, Turkey; Beirut, Lebanon; Athens, Greece; Brussels, Belgium; and London, England.

In Istanbul I wanted to see two places: the ancient church of Hagia (Saint) Sophia, which was constructed in the 5th Century during the rules of Byzantine Romans, and the Ottoman palaces that were constructed during the Middle Ages. In the distant past the Romans and Ottomans waged many battles with the Persians, which made these places of historical interest to me. I found Istanbul a very attractive city because on one side it was Europe and on the other side Asia, an interesting mixture of cultures. As yet there were not many tall buildings to obscure the views of the beautiful churches and palaces. The most sought after place to go at night was on the top of the Hilton hotel, which was overlooking the Bosphorus and Black Sea with the lights of cruise ships shining on the Bosphorus. The entertainment on the top of the hotel included Turkish food and drinks, accompanied by Turkish music. The atmosphere was gay and the place was full of attractive people.

My next destination was Beirut, Lebanon. The main reason for my going there was to visit one of my uncles and his family who were living there. It was a joyous occasion to see my uncle whom I greatly loved. He treated me royally and showed me many beautiful sites in Beirut, especially the beaches that were full of attractive foreign young ladies wearing bikinis. Lebanon is a Moslem country, but at the time of my visit, there appeared to be a strong international culture by allowing chadors and bikinis to mix. I am glad that I saw Beirut in its happy days because later Beirut radically changed when the Palestinians moved there. The international culture was replaced with the Moslem customs and frequent fights with the Israel which destroyed much of the city.

For my last night entertainment, my uncle and his wife drove me to a top of a hill outside the city. From there I could see the lights of the city. There was an old fashioned restaurant on the top of the hill. The sound of falling water from a stream crossing the hill provided natural music. At the bank of the stream, carpets were spread for us to sit down. After we sat down, the servants spread a large cover sheet in front of us and began to serve us dishes of delicious Lebanese delicacies. My uncle said these are not dinner, but Lebanese meze (hors d'oeuvres). They kept bringing one after another until the cover sheet became full of dishes, maybe around 30. I asked my uncle please do not order any dinner, because the dishes they have already served us are far greater than my capacity to eat.

From Beirut I flew to Athens, Greece, the site of many battles between Persians and Grecians over two thousand years ago. My brief visit was focused on visiting the Parthenon, where in ancient past the Greek scholars gathered to discuss a range of subjects, like politics, sciences, history, philosophy, art, and so forth. Despite all the damages, such as the taking of all the marbles by the British, the building still remained a masterpiece of architecture, something that has been copied by many countries in the West. At night it stood illuminated on the top of a hill above the city to remind the visitors of being the home of progress in human knowledge in the age of antiquity.

After Beirut my final destinations, before going to Boston, were Brussels and London. I went to Brussels because a Belgian friend had invited me to show me the Belgium countryside by traveling on the back of her motorcycle. It was indeed a great adventure and a learning experience about the Belgian people. For example, it was a new experience for me to stay in several-hundred-year-old inns and observe the old customs and traditions. Finally I went to London to catch up with my friends from Harvard and be on time for the Harvard chartered flight to Boston. I just had enough time to spend a few hours in the British Museum to see the historic Persian relics. In particular, I wanted to see the cylinder of Cyrus the Great, where, as the king of Persia, he was the first world leader to declare his respect for human rights, including race and religion. This was over two thousand years before anyone else made such a declaration.

10 Creating My American Family

In my last year in Philadelphia I took a date to the Philadelphia Opera. After the opera my date invited me to come to her house in Chestnut Hill because her brother was having a party. When I arrived at her house I saw a group of young ladies sitting around the fire, but their dates, somewhat drunk, were roughhousing on the porch. It turned out that all the girls were students at Wellesley College in suburban Boston and the boys were students at Dartmouth College in New Hampshire. I immediately became a hit with the girls because they all were bored with their dates and I was a handsome, well-dressed, young doctor, who had just taken his date to see a great opera. The girls surrounded me to find out who I was.

Among the girls that I met, the one who impressed me the

most was Joan Foedisch. She had come to Philadelphia to spend a school holiday with her grandparents, Buzz and Dorothy Jellett, who also lived in Chestnut Hill. I told her I am shortly coming to Boston for my postgraduate medical training and, therefore, I would like to get to know her. Later I met her grandparents in their elegant house in Chestnut Hill. I was warmly greeted by Joan's grandparents in their grand entrance hall that was beautifully designed. They were very charming, had travelled in many places, and the grandmother turned out to be an expert on the opera. They were among the social elites in Philadelphia. Needless to say, I was greatly impressed.

Soon after I moved to Boston, I called Joan to tell her I'd like to come to see Wellesley College because I want to evaluate whether it is a suitable school for my niece, Goli Hamedi. Her mother, my sister Faranak, had written me a letter from Iran asking me to find a school for my niece in Boston and to serve as her guardian. Joan gladly invited me to come to see her for a tour of her college. This led to the beginning of a dating relationship. I learned that she was born in Philadelphia eight years after I was born in Tehran. Her parents, George and Clara Foedisch, moved to Pittsburgh when she was nine years old because her father wanted to set up an insurance company there. Apparently this was a hard decision because Joan's parents were celebrities in the social circles in Philadelphia. Her father, George, was a Princeton University graduate and champion in sports like squash, tennis, and golf. Her mother, Clara, was a top of the line debutante, squash and tennis player and a great horseback rider in Philadelphia. Fortunately, they were able to transfer their social prominence from Philadelphia to Sewickley, a beautiful suburb north of Pittsburgh where they joined clubs and made many friends in the community.

The move necessitated a change in school for Joan. She had to leave the Springside School in Chestnut Hill, a girls only school which she liked very much and where she had many friends, and enter Sewickley Academy, a private coed school. Although she was not happy with the move, she soon began to like Sewickley Academy and made many good friends there. In Sewickley Academy her main sport was tennis in which she excelled to become a top player in the Junior Wightman Cup. After finishing Sewickley Academy, her parents sent her to Abbot Academy boarding school that is located outside of Boston. After she graduated from Abbot, the school became part of the Phillips Andover Academy, which is next door to Abbot.

When she was a freshman in Wellesley College, Joan's parents presented her to the Pittsburgh social elites in the Cinderella Ball as a debutante. Apparently, she enjoyed the debutante parties, especially those held at the Mellon estate in Ligonier.

Joan at age of 18 as a debutante for presentation at the Cinderella Ball in Pittsburgh.

As time went on my relationship with Joan became more serious because we realized we had common interests. For example, we both liked the Boston Symphony, going to theaters, dining in interesting cafes, and even traveling to New York to see my favorite operas at the Metropolitan Opera. Therefore, it was natural for me to begin to think that I might have found the right person to be my wife. To verify this I thought I should show Joan to my first friend in America, Gene Galen, who had become my roommate at Johns Hopkins University. One of his advice to me was to search for a Wellesley girl if I decide to get married. He thought the Wellesley girls make the best wives for men who wanted to be successful. Fortunately, my old roommate was living in Boston and doing advanced medical training. He and his wife were delighted to invite me and Joan to their Boston apartment for dinner. They were both very impressed with Joan. Gene cornered me in his study to tell me that I had found the right girl and I should go for it.

The advice of my old roommate and trusting friend and meeting my family expectations firmed up my will to propose to Joan. Besides Gene Galen's advice I had to honor my family rules for marrying. First, she had to be from a noble family. Secondly, she had to be well-educated. Third, she had to be good looking and well mannered. Joan highly met the above criteria. However, when I proposed she felt that she was not yet prepared to make the commitment. She reasoned that I was her first serious boyfriend and she needed time to get experience with other men to know what kind of man she wanted to spend the rest of her life with. She also wanted to go to graduate school in social work and did not know how this would be affected by being married. Lastly she was concerned with what would be the reaction of the social elites of Sewickley if they hear that she has married a Persian. Nobody there knew much about Persia and probably thought that Persians were Arab barbarians.

This discussion took place in June of 1962 when she graduated from Wellesley College. I thought her indecision necessitated for us to be separated for a while to let her think about our relationship. Therefore, in the summer of 1962, as I described in the previous chapter, was the time that I also decided to take a trip to Iran and find out what is the best option for me, namely, moving back to Iran after twelve years of being away or staying in America. If the decision was to move back, I could no longer pursue Joan.

Joan had already decided to leave me by moving to Philadelphia to study for a Master in Social Work at Bryn Mawr College. However, I kept sending her postcards from all the cities in the Middle East and Europe that I visited (see previous chapter) with a brief account of my adventures. She later told me that each time she received my postcard she got upset that she was not accompanying me in such an exciting travel tour.

When I came back from my trip, I called her in Philadelphia to say I am back. From the phone call I sensed that she had missed me while I was gone. This encouraged me to try to see her again. Therefore, I invited her to come back to Boston for a weekend, which she immediately accepted. She was impressed with my new elegant apartment just off the Harvard Bridge. The Harvard Bridge connects Cambridge to the Back Bay area in Boston. Since at that time I was spending a lot more time at MIT than at Harvard hospitals, it was an ideal location for me. In fact, I could see MIT buildings and the Charles River from the windows of my apartment.

When Joan arrived in Boston, I took her to dinner in a nice restaurant that was located on the first floor of my building. After the meal and a glass of wine, I felt the courage to ask her again whether she would marry me. She immediately said yes, but with conditions. She took a piece of paper and wrote ten conditions for me to sign. To bring a little humor, I wrote   on her paper that "I surrender" and accept all her conditions. We agreed to have an engagement party during the Christmas holiday in Sewickley to make the announcement.

Joan's parents were anxious to meet me, but had to wait until Christmas. They had accepted Joan's decision to marry me, but were curious to find out why Joan chose me over others. Their concern dissipated when they saw I was a smash hit with the Sewickley crowd. In fact, a prominent business leader of Pittsburgh, who was the president of the Oliver Reality, tried to encourage me to move to Pittsburgh by promising to endow a research foundation for me. After the engagement, we kept in touch for the next six months by either Joan's coming to visit me in Boston or my going to Philadelphia to visit her. Finally, we reached June 15, 1963, the announced date of our wedding. Before flying to Pittsburgh, I began to have concerns about getting through all the wedding rituals they had planned in Sewickley. However, my mood completely changed when I got there and saw how warmly Joan's parents' friends had opened up their houses to accommodate me and my relatives and friends.

My relatives and friends, who had come from all over the world, were already there and having a great time. The rehearsal dinner was planned to be held in the Edgeworth Club and our wedding ceremony at Saint Stephen's Episcopal Church, all in Sewickley. Joan and I planned all the details of our wedding service. For example, we had asked a friend of ours from Philadelphia to sing arias from the Handel's Messiah and asked a friend of ours who was the head of the religious department at Exeter in Massachusetts and also an Episcopal minister to officiate at our wedding. The wedding reception was to be held on the lawn of Joan's parents' big house in Sewickley. The weather turned out to be ideal and all the plans were carried out perfectly. I was so greatly enjoying the wedding festivities with my dear relatives and close friends that when time came to leave for our honeymoon I did not want to depart.

Our picture taken the night before our wedding, usually called the rehearsal dinner. (My bride looks very happy and adoring.)

For our honeymoon we chose a French-style resort on a beautiful lake outside of Quebec City, Canada. We chose this place because it was like going to an old part of Europe. It had everything we wanted such as trails for hiking, swimming, tennis, horseback riding, etc. The food was excellent French cuisine and at night, it was served on a patio with the view of the lake and sounds of romantic music. On the first morning of our honeymoon, my wife woke me up early and said, "Let's go practice tennis." She was a great tennis player because since the time when she was able to hold a racket her parents had put pressure on her to play tennis. In contrast my tennis experience was limited to playing a few times in a tennis club in Tehran when I was a teenager. In view of my wife's great love for tennis, I felt that I had to learn it. She spent a great deal of time teaching me until I became competitive with her.

However, this took several months of trying.

I thought I should return her favor of teaching me tennis, by teaching her some sport that I was good at. For this reason I introduced her to horseback riding. Unfortunately, after we left Quebec we no longer had access to a horse to continue teaching her.

Joan was happy to get back to Boston to live and go to school. I was happy not commuting to Philadelphia to see her. During the first year of our marriage when she was going to Boston University for her Master in Social Work she became pregnant. This necessitated our moving to a larger apartment. The apartment we selected was located in a beautiful area of Boston called Brookline. The apartment had a big living, dining, bed, and guest rooms.

There was also a small room for my office and a big porch for sitting outside. There was also a nice park with tennis courts outside of our apartment.

Joan gave birth to a healthy baby on the day of our first wedding anniversary. The baby was a handsome boy and we named him David, which is Davud in Persian.

When David was four and a half months old a great tragedy darkened our happy life.

One morning after we woke up Joan went to our son's room to feed him. She was shocked to find him dead. Apparently, during the night he suffered a crib death, which no one still knows the cause of it.

Needless to say, we were devastated and kept blaming ourselves. The funeral service was planned for the Old Advent Church in the Beacon Hill section of Boston and was attended by a large number of our friends and colleagues, including my MIT and Harvard chairmen and Joan's parents. This was the first and last time I saw Joan's father cry.

To take our minds off the tragedy we drove a friend's car across the country, from Boston to Seattle and then to San Francisco. Joan was seven months pregnant. The trip was full of adventures and we were also awed with the vastness of our country and its many great natural beauties. After a few days in California visiting friends we flew back from Los Angeles to Boston. We left the car in San Francisco for our friend, the owner of the car, who was coming to live there.

In the fall of 1965 our second child was born in Boston. We named her Elise and became busy taking care of her. The fear of crib death made us become very protective and watchful of her.

Soon after the birth of our daughter, I began to spend time thinking about our future because in June 1966 I was scheduled to receive my Ph.D. in nutritional sciences and physiological chemistry from MIT and was also completing my medical training at the Peter Bent Brigham Hospital of Harvard Medical School. At that time Harvard Medical School had very few tenured professorship positions. Therefore, all they could offer me was a position of being Harvard Ambassador to their nutritional projects around the world. The position involved a lot of traveling, and no guarantee of a future tenure and therefore not suitable to my needs. Firstly, I did not want to be away from my young family and secondly, I wanted to be on a tenure-track professorship. My Harvard friends suggested that I should contact Jack Myers, the legendary chairman of medicine at the University of Pittsburgh. He was formerly at Harvard and was looking for a chief of gastroenterology. He was happy to see me and offered me a full time position in his department and with the promise that if I performed well, in three years I would be offered a tenured professorship.

It was such a good offer that I could not refuse. In addition,

I wanted our children to grow in close proximity to their grandparents. I thought this would be important for our children to get to know their grandparents well and enjoy their affections. However, my wife was not enthusiastic about leaving Boston, because we had developed very warm and close relationships with many Bostonian friends. To lessen my wife's reservation for leaving Boston I promised her to build a summerhouse in the Cape Cod area of Massachusetts. I assured her that we would use this house to come back every summer and invite our Bostonian friends to come see us.

Before we settled in Pittsburgh, we thought of taking a summer trip in Europe. Neither of us had been to any country in Scandinavia. Therefore, we planned to go to Denmark, Sweden, and Norway. A relative of ours offered his car in Europe for us to drive across Scandinavia. This enabled us to see a great number of beautiful and historic places of the three countries and become familiar with many local cultures and customs. As far as the natural beauty and way of life was concerned, we liked Norway the best.

In the fall of 1966, we moved to Pittsburgh and bought a house in an area called Squirrel Hill. Our house was in a very close proximity to educational places like the Chatham College, Carnegie Mellon University, and the University of Pittsburgh. We found the cultural offerings, like concerts, operas, plays, actually richer than in Boston and by joining The Pittsburgh Golf Club, which was only three blocks away from our house, we had access to the best sports and dining facilities in the country. Gradually, we began to enjoy our life in Pittsburgh and thought we made a very good choice by moving to this city. In fact, we were not alone thinking this way because a number of times the Rand Corporation surveys of the cities in America have shown Pittsburgh to be "the most livable city."

Soon after we settled in Pittsburgh, our family began to grow. In a span of short time, my wife gave birth to two additional wonderful babies – one boy and one girl. We named them Camron and Jennifer, respectively.

Shortly after we settled in Pittsburgh we began to search for a suitable place for building our summer house in the eastern shore of Massachusetts. One of our friends in New England suggested that we should visit the little island of Chappaquiddick that is in the Atlantic Ocean about 9 miles away from the mainland. In fact, when we visited the island in the summer of 1969, we immediately were convinced that we had found the right place for our summer home. The island was far more rural than any place on Cape Cod; there were miles of spectacular beaches with many shore birds, but with very few people. The Gulfstream by flowing between the Chappaquiddick Island and Nantucket Island kept the water adequately warm to allow enjoyable swimming.

We made an extensive search of the island looking for a property that best met what we liked. We finally decided on a location called Sampson's Hill, which is the highest point on the island and has also the greatest historical significance. For example, in earlier times it hosted a one-room cabin as the meeting house and was used to send telegraphic messages across the Atlantic Ocean and monitor the Nantucket Sound for the possible appearance of enemy ships during World War II. Finally, perhaps the most important reason for selecting our location was that the people on the island told us that there never would be any house built in our front view, which showed 8 miles of lush forests, and then Nantucket Sound and its Island. The reason was that all the forests in our front view were in conservation and therefore not buildable. After building our summer house for enjoying sociability and sailing, we joined the Edgartown Yacht Club. To get to Edgartown we can either take a ferry or go by my motor boat, which is moored on a Chappaquiddick beach. The Yacht Club was founded in late 19th Century and provides the best summer teaching programs for children in sailing and tennis. We also have to go often to Edgartown because of our needs for shopping since there are no shops on the Chappaquiddick.

Initially, because of my work in the Pittsburgh Medical Center, I was commuting between our winter and summer houses, but our children always spent the whole summer on the island and had a great time. They all became excellent sailors and won many trophies by participating in the races organized by the Edgartown Yacht Club. They began to win these trophies during the 1970's when they were all teenagers. Furthermore, the director of the sailing program was so impressed with Jennifer's sailing skills that he asked her to become the teacher of the adult sailing classes.

Our children still love to come to Chappaquiddick for their summer vacations. We greatly enjoy seeing our children going swimming, sailing, and playing tennis and other pleasure activities. Recently there have been additions to our family summer gathering in Chappaquiddick. Jennifer and our son-in-law David Teoste have given us three wonderful grandchildren named Axelrein, Lucinda, and Cyrus, whom they bring along. Like their parents they are also enthusiastic about our summer place.

We have greatly expanded our initial property. We bought three more properties that were adjacent to our initial property. We have given one of them to the Sheriff's Meadow Foundation to be kept in a permanent conservation trust. The other two properties we have kept untouched and are saving them for our children if they want to build their own summerhouse. Building on Chappaquiddick is very expensive and, at present, they cannot afford to do it, but, hopefully, in the future when their economic status improves, they can fulfill their dreams.

Early after building our house, I realized we needed to have a mooring for our sailboat and a private beach for our water activities. I found that all the moorings in the inner harbor close to our house belonged to island people. Again I got lucky and found a neighbor who was getting too old to go sailing; therefore, he no longer needed his mooring. He offered to sell it to me. His mooring was located in an ideal location and I immediately bought it. The search for a private beach turned out to be more difficult. There were very few available and those available were extremely expensive. I solved this problem by joining with few of our friends to form an association to buy a private beach. The beach is spectacular. It is located on outer Edgartown Harbor with a great view of the sailboats moving around either for pleasure or racing. Our beach is next to the famous Chappy Beach Club, which was shown in the movie "Jaws." We have a perfect sandy beach for swimming. We have built platforms for keeping our small boats like kayaks, windsurfers, etc., on the beach that we also use for giving beach parties.

In retrospect, my decision to use the money I inherited from the estate of my father in Iran to buy properties and build a summerhouse on the Chappaquiddick has proved to be a great foresight. For over 40 years my family and I have greatly benefited from the wide variety of offerings of this beautiful and unique island.

When I reached middle age, I began to consider myself a very lucky person. I had everything I wanted in life – a great wife, three wonderful and highly intelligent children, a very successful career (to be described in the next chapter), top of the line social privileges, and a rich life of pleasures and possessions. This led me to think of changing my lifestyle by spending more time with my family, particularly my wife. To do this I needed to greatly reduce the time spent at the university and my traveling across the U.S. and around the world. I was getting ready to propose to her that we spend more time doing things together, when suddenly and unexpectedly, she brought down the roof on me by announcing that she planned to move out of our house and live in an apartment by herself. I could not believe this was happening and when I realized she was serious, I was devastated. The unexpected sudden death of my mother (described in Chapter 4) and the unexpected sudden breakdown of my marriage are the most traumatic experiences of my life that I have gone through because, in both cases, I loved them each intensely and was so dependent on each of them. At first I blamed myself for not paying enough attention to her by keeping so busy at work, but later I realized there were also many other complex reasons for the breakdown of our marriage.

Living alone also was very hard for me and appeared to be the same for her because she regularly checked up on me. After a year of separation, we jointly made the decision to get back together. This was in 1988. During the subsequent years we both have come to the firm conviction that we need each other and there can never be again a possibility of separation.

Finally, the most recent picture of my American family taken on Christmas day of 2013 is shown below.

From left to right, seated: my daughter, Jennifer, holding her daughter, Lucy, me, my wife, Joan, my daughter, Elise, holding her nephew Axel. Standing, my son, Camron, my son-in-law, David Teoste, (Jennifer's husband) holding his son, Cyrus.

11 Educating Our Children

My own experience of childhood played a major role in raising our children. I convinced my wife that we should allow our children the freedom of making their own decisions as much as possible. Because I had enjoyed this privilege and it had worked well for me, I thought I should pass it on to my children. For example, when our son Camron was a little boy he decided to earn money by delivering morning newspapers. Despite my worries for his health and safety to go out in the dark and bitter cold to deliver newspapers, I could not bring myself to oppose him.

For choosing kindergarten and elementary school, we had to decide because our children were too young. We had ideal schools from which to choose. For the kindergarten we chose the Shady Lane School and for the elementary school we chose the Wightman School. Our children liked our selections, in particular the Wightman School, because it was a block away from our house and they could easily come home for lunch. We listened to our children's preferences about their schooling. Elise expressed interest in going to a new experimental public school located in a predominantly African-American neighborhood. She wanted to go because the other children in our neighborhood were going. After much discussion and consultation with our friends and neighbors, my wife and I decided that despite the long bus ride, we would send Elise to East Hills. It was the early 1970's and we wanted to support racial integration in the public schools. Elise valued the experience she had at this school even though it was difficult for her, especially since she was so petite.

After that we let our children decide their schools. Elise tried just about every variety of educational experience possible until she found the perfect school for herself. After public school she tried an all-girls private school. It was very strict and she became rebellious. After trying another public school, she asked if she could go to boarding school. At age 14 in 1979 she took a Greyhound bus by herself to go investigate several boarding schools. She immediately fell in love with the Putney School in Vermont. Putney was the progressive and utopian school Elise had been looking for. The students called their teachers by their first names, they were not graded and they had school meetings every day. It was a working dairy farm and the students were required to do farm work. Putney gave Elise the foundation she was looking for, and she went on to excel academically and artistically. After Putney and after two years at the University of Pittsburgh, she was accepted at Swarthmore College, where she graduated with an Honors major in Philosophy.

After Swarthmore Elise moved to Boston, the City of her birth. She got a job in an architecture office and discovered her love of architecture. She went to the University of Pennsylvania and received a Master of Architecture. In architecture school her creativity flourished and she was encouraged by her professors to pursue her artistic vision. She moved to New York after school to work in architecture, but it was during this period that she realized that her calling was to be an artist. Becoming an artist was not what I wanted to hear. I knew how difficult it would be for her to sustain herself, but she persisted. After several years trying to do architecture and art and having several "day jobs" she decided she needed to go back to school. She earned a Masters of Fine Arts degree at Columbia University.

Elise has a deep commitment to her work and her path as an artist has been full of challenges. Many of the challenges have been financial. I have always believed in my daughter's talent and I am one of her biggest fans. I am also one of her biggest collectors. Both of my houses, in Pittsburgh and Chappaquiddick are filled with her work from her different periods. Elise has needed substantial financial support from my wife and me to sustain her career path. Although it has not been easy for her parents, it is very gratifying now to know that we have helped her to realize her dreams.

Her art accomplishments include the following:

(1) She has served as an assistant professor of painting at Columbia University and at the Brooklyn College after she got her MFA degree (Master of Fine Art) from Columbia in 2007.

(2) In 2007 she was awarded a fellowship by the Terra foundation to work with an international group of painters in Giverny, France (the village of the famous French painter, Claude Monet

(3) In 2008 she received a grant from the Pollock-Krasner Foundation to develop her paintings.

(4) In 2009 she curated "Gold in Braddock," an exhibition of seventeen national artists in Pittsburgh.

(5) In 2010 she had a solo exhibition at Southfirst Gallery in Brooklyn, which was reviewed in the most respected art journal called *Art Forum.*

(6) In 2011 her paintings were exhibited in the Andy Warhol Museum for several months.

(7) In 2012 she had a solo exhibit in the Churner and Churner Gallery in Manhattan, New York City.

(8) In 2013 she had her big honor to be asked to show her paintings in the New York City at The Armory Show on the occasion of its centennial anniversary.

(9) After the Armory exhibition, she was invited to serve as a scholar fellow in art at the Radcliffe Institute for Advanced Study of the Harvard University for a full academic year with all expenses paid (like a MacArthur grant).

(10) Shortly after the Harvard offer she was honored with her second Pollock-Krasner Foundation grant to continue with her painting contribution to the art world.

(11) Most recently she had an exhibition of her paintings in the art gallery of the Radcliffe Institute. She titled the exhibit "Metabolic Paintings," and it was reviewed in *The Boston Globe* as well as fully reported in the January issue 2014 of *Artforum*.

(12) Her future plans include an exhibition of her recent paintings in New York City and teaching again at Brooklyn College. It gives me great joy that after so many years of persistence, Elise's painting is being recognized and appreciated. It also makes me incredibly happy to see my daughter doing what she loves, and knowing that I played a big part in making that possible.

Our second child, Camron, after finishing elementary school, chose an elite private school for boys called the St. Edmund's Academy in Pittsburgh. St. Edmund's Academy was very close to our house. Camron did well there. For example, he became a favorite student of the school headmaster Sterling Miller. Unfortunately, the school ended by the 9th grade. He then chose to go to Shadyside Academy, which is a very well-endowed school with a beautiful campus and with all kinds of sport facilities. However, Camron was not happy with his choice because the school was located in the suburbs of Pittsburgh and he, therefore, had a long commute. He was exhausted after sports and had no time or energy for studying. He developed a liking for the boarding school from which his sister had graduated. We therefore sent him to the Putney School in Vermont to finish his high school, which he greatly liked.

After graduating from the Putney School he told us he needed to get away from the family to find himself. He moved to the mountains of Colorado to think and ponder on his life and future. He was attracted to Colorado because he could be close to wilderness and sports that he greatly liked such as skiing, rafting, kayaking, and ice climbing and particularly rafting and kayaking on the Colorado River. He never asked us for money. He always found employment.

Finally, he came to the conclusion that he liked the outdoor environment the best and would like to develop skills to contribute to its protection and maintenance. He enrolled himself in the Mesa State College in Grand Junction, Colorado, to earn a bachelor of science degree in environmental restoration and waste management. He graduated with magna cum laude recognition and nomination to the National College Honor Society.

After graduation he worked for a while in Grand Junction with agencies like the U.S. Geological Survey, Nature Conservancy, and Long-Range Planning Department. These experiences convinced him that he needed more education. He returned to Pittsburgh and enrolled himself for a master of science degree in sustainable design from the Carnegie Mellon University School of Architecture, which is one of the best in the country. After graduation he was recruited by New York companies working on greening old buildings, wastewater management, and sustainable strategies for new construction.

A couple of years ago he realized that there is a crisis in water pollution in the Martha's Vineyard. In contrast to the mainland, the island depends solely on water in its aquifers, pond, and beaches. Aquifers are used for drinking water and ponds and beaches are used for fishing. All these bodies of water have become seriously affected by sewage and chemical pollutants. Because of his love for the Martha's Vineyard he decided to move there and try to apply his expertise to solving the water problems. Thus far the authorities on the island have been reluctant to believe the evidence for the pollution of the island water, despite the presence of clear evidence such as the disappearance of shellfish and fish from the island waters. However, his youthful passion for saving the island from these environmental disasters has been recognized by the members of the conservation boards and the editorial board of the *Vineyard Gazette*, which is the leading newspaper. He has been invited to join the board of the Vineyard Conservation Society and you can read his editorial of past years in the *Vineyard Gazette* (e.g., Nov. 18, 2011 and Aug. 2, 2011).

Currently he is working to clean up pollution in the harbor of Gloucester, Massachusetts. Gloucester was the center of fishing that has now disappeared causing great economic hardship to the town. Camron has proposed methods for greening the Gloucester Harbor, but needs financial support to go ahead with the project.

I greatly admire Elise's serious commitment to art and Camron's commitment to preserving fishing and water quality. However, in view of our present economy and cutbacks, I am not sure that they will be adequately supported for their efforts in enhancing art and the environment by the government and the public. Therefore, I have agreed to support them financially as long as they need it.

Our last child, Jennifer, is a graduate of the Ellis School in Pittsburgh, which is a private girl's school. During her high school years she became a strong advocate of world peace by joining the Fellowship of Reconciliation. She also initiated publishing a newspaper for her school, covering the news and politics. Furthermore, she travelled with the Fellowship group to Russia to promote peace when the Communists were in power.

When George Bush in 1991 declared his intention to attack Iraq, we all became very concerned and wrote many letters to the White House voicing our strong opposition to military action. Unfortunately, we got no response. Jennifer, realizing that George Bush was not going to listen to our advice, decided, with the help of the Fellowship of Reconciliation organization, to organize a peace group to go to Iraq to persuade Sadam Hussein to avoid war by agreeing to George Bush's demand to leave Kuwait alone.

We were opposed to Jennifer risking her life by going to Iraq, but she was determined.

Consequently, we became a hot subject for the national media. Television cameras surrounded our house to keep up with the news of Jennifer and her group's progress in Baghdad. I kept telling them that I have no news from her. The public concern escalated leading to organizing a church vigil to pray for the safe return of Jennifer and her group. This appeared to me like a memorial service and I became tearful. Fortunately, the King of Jordan learned that the American attack was imminent and ordered the Jordanian Royal Airline to immediately fly Jennifer and her group to New York. Six hours after their departure, the America Air Force began to bomb Baghdad. After arrival in the U.S., she was interviewed on national news for her experience in Baghdad. We were overjoyed with her safe return.

After graduating from the Ellis School, she entered Brown University for her college education. Before graduation, she began to campaign for a need-blind admission policy. She and a group of students had to take over the office of the university president for a sit-down strike to make the school agree to need-blind admission. The president called the police and Jennifer and her group were arrested. I was outraged with the action of the president for calling the police and I called him to express my anger. The students were released the next day.

At graduation I was invited to the home of the president, Vartan Gregorian (born in Iran), for a reception. I found him to be a very charming person and we became friends. At Brown Jennifer majored in Russian studies and became very knowledgeable about Russia and very fluent in its language.

To put what she had learned at Brown to work, Jennifer moved to Russia for two years and worked on getting the grass-root people to clear their environment from pollution. She eventually was advanced to become a director of U.S.-Russian Environmental Program.

After returning from Russia, she continued her work on the effects of pollutants, but this time not on the environment, but on humans. To get training for such work, she enrolled in a master's degree program at Columbia University School of Public Health. For her research project she chose to study the effects of a pollutant like phthalates, a compound found in plastics and personal care products, on the placental development in early pregnancy and on placental-fetal interactions. The results of these studies have been published in issues of the American Journal of Epidemiology (169(8):1015-1024, 2009). and Environmental Health Perspective

(PMCID 21893441, 2011).

She did so well at Columbia that Harvard University offered her a full scholarship with her living expenses to join the Department of Environmental Health as a doctoral candidate. To finish her epidemiological studies at Harvard she stayed for one additional year as a post-doctoral fellow after she received her doctoral degree in 2007.

In 2008 she moved to the west coast to join the Department of Obstetrics and Gynecology in the School of Medicine of the University of California in San Francisco (UCSF) as a post-doctoral scholar.

Soon after she began her post-doctoral fellowship, Jennifer was awarded a much sought after training grant from the National Institutes of Health to cover her research expenses and salary for five years (R01). The grant allowed Jennifer to take the grant with her to whichever university she decided to move to. She has used this grant to do pioneering studies on the effect of phthalates on the placenta at the molecular level after becoming a molecular biologist.

In 2013 Jennifer finished three years of fellowship at UCSF (University of California at San Francisco) and was promoted to the position of Assistant Professor in the Department of Obstetrics and Gynecology. However, she needed to find a tenure-track position. So she started a job search. Several other universities offered her a faculty position, but she became most impressed with the offer she received from the University of Pittsburgh. As a result, she is currently a member of the Department of Epidemiology in the School of Public Health and a member of the Department of Obstetrics and Gynecology in the School of Medicine. She considered Pittsburgh an excellent place for her own growth in academic medicine and for the growth of her three children by being near their grandparents.

Her husband since 2006, David Teoste, has agreed to give up his job as a geologist and look after the three children while Jennifer is busy establishing her research and teaching programs at the University of Pittsburgh.

In conclusion my wife and I are very proud of our three

children. They have grown to be outstanding citizens by being responsible, thoughtful, and caring. They have excelled in their chosen professions and are making great contributions to advancing art, environmental protection, and medical science in their country.

12 Rescuing University Medical Center from Disintegration

My coming to Pittsburgh required commitments of support for my clinical and research activities. My activities needed sufficient space for office and research laboratories and the hiring of a secretary, a research assistant, teaching faculty members, and research support until I could get funded for my grant applications. These were needed because prior to my arrival there was no academic program in gastroenterology. There were a only a few gastroenterologists who took care of gastrointestinal problems of patients in the affiliated hospitals of the university. It turned out that Jack Myers, the legendary chairman of Medicine, had no space and money to meet my needs, but he had a solution. He told me that Montefiore Hospital had joined the university as a teaching hospital of the University. The hospital did have money and space to meet my needs. In return I could help them to advance the status of the hospital as a prominent university teaching and research center. Since my salary was going to be paid by the university I would be responsible for teaching gastroenterology to the medical students and doctors in training. As a result, I was spread out through the University Medical Center. I had my gastroenterology Clinic and basic research laboratories at Montefiore Hospital. My patients for clinical research were admitted to Presbyterian Hospital. I would see patients on consultation at Presbyterian and Children's Hospital.

Montefiore Hospital is across the street from the medical school and Presbyterian and Children's Hospitals and a block away from Magee-Women's Hospital. Therefore, it is very convenient for interaction and collaboration among these institutions. Originally, Montefiore Hospital was built several decades earlier to allow

Jewish doctors, who could not get admitting privileges at the Presbyterian Hospital, to admit their patients to a hospital of their own. During these years the hospital was run by the Jewish practicing physicians. Therefore, when Montefiore Hospital became a university hospital, the practicing physicians revolted for being put under the authority of the university-appointed full time chiefs of services like me. The revolt was very heated, emotional, and unpleasant. However, the trustees of Montefiore Hospital persisted in their decision to convert their community hospital to a university hospital and finally they prevailed. This resulted in ill feelings from a group of Jewish doctors toward Montefiore Hospital.

The design of the UPMC organization, which was largely influenced by Jack Myers' experience at Harvard, was to have Presbyterian, Montefiore, Children's, and Magee Women's hospitals each run by its own trustees, but all under the academic direction of the medical school. This operational design was in effect until Jack Myers retired. Unfortunately, after he gave up his position of power and influence at the medical school, the chief of surgical and medical services at the Presbyterian Hospital began to attack the autonomy of Montefiore Hospital. Under the leadership of Hank Bahnson, the aggressive chairman of the department of surgery, they demanded that the chiefs of services at Montefiore Hospital be put under the command of the chiefs of services in Presbyterian hospital. The reasons for the demand included the chairman's desire for increasing his power and having access to the space and financial assets of Montefiore Hospital. To give teeth to their demand, Bahnson issued an ultimatum that if Montefiore would not accept the demand, the hospital will be kicked out as a member of the University Health Center. All this caused a great crisis in the viability of the health center and became of great concern to the public. The trustees of Montefiore were getting nowhere with their persuasion of the Presbyterian chiefs to withdraw their demands.

I decided to personally step into the battle of rescuing the University Medical Center from coming apart. I informed the trustees of the Montefiore Hospital that I am a close friend of the chairman of the board of the University trustees, Bill Rea, and I could take their arguments for keeping the Montefiore hospital autonomous directly to him. The reason I knew Bill Rea so well was because my wife had grown up with his family and Joan's father, George Foedisch, and Bill Rea were classmates at Princeton University. The Montefiore trustees were very happy to learn of my connection to the University board chairman. At my request they prepared for me a long list of arguments for allowing Montefiore to remain as an autonomous member of the University Health Center. When I called Bill Rea to discuss the health center crisis he immediately invited me to the Harvard Yale Princeton (HYP) club for lunch. We had several of these lunches and several hours of discussion, but finally I succeeded to convince him of the validity of my arguments. When the chairman and CEO of Montefiore heard news of my success, they became very happy and pleased with my saving them. In fact, as a reward they offered to convert a whole wing of the hospital as state-of-art offices and laboratories for me and my staff.

Unfortunately, a few years later another crisis hit Montefiore Hospital. This time the crisis was a financial decline. This was caused by a great fall of inpatient admissions to the hospital. The unhappy Jewish doctors, instead of taking pride in the success of their hospital, began to use non-Jewish hospitals for admitting their patients. Apparently, the prejudice against Jewish doctors was no longer a problem and they could admit their patients to any Pittsburgh hospital they wanted. In face of Montefiore hospital's approaching bankruptcy because of loss of patients, its trustees were compelled to sell Montefiore Hospital to Presbyterian Hospital. Currently, both hospitals have a common trustee and the Montefiore faculties were reassigned. The money from the sale of the hospital was used to create a Jewish Charitable Foundation.

13 Research and Practice

This chapter is to give a summary of my contributions to advancing science in the practice of medicine. In 1966 I moved to Pittsburgh to setup the University's first academic program in gastroenterology (GI). Although the Department of Medicine at

Pitt was only interested in the gastroenterology, I persuaded them to allow me to also include clinical nutrition in my program. This was the first time anywhere in the U.S. that a medical school included clinical nutrition in its formal curriculum. I had thought about this when I was at MIT working toward a doctorate in nutritional science.

The group includes research physicians, basic scientists and research technicians.

Shortly after I arrived in Pittsburgh, I began to get consults to see patients with GI and nutritional problems. I initiated a series of lectures on gastroenterology and nutrition as a part of the introduction to medicine course for the sophomore medical students. For the senior students and medical residents I offered a six-week training in my clinical service and two years of fellowship training for producing future gastroenterologists and nutritionists. To help me with my clinical responsibilities I hired a group of well-educated faculty members with expertise either in gastroenterology or in nutrition. As far as my research programs were concerned, I hired a large staff of research associates, research fellows, and research technicians.

My research interests covered three different areas. The first one dealt with the intestinal absorption of the products of protein digestion. These studies invalidated the long-term belief that only amino acids could be absorbed. We showed that, in fact, there is absorption of dipeptides and tripeptides, which are more efficiently absorbed than amino acids. Therefore, the intestinal assimilation of dietary proteins is mainly in the form of peptides rather than in amino acid form.

The second one dealt with the regulation of metabolism of three essential amino acids (leucine, isoleucine, and valine) which are large components of dietary proteins. These studies opened a new era in the metabolic regulation.

The third one dealt with the treatment of human obesity. I was the first to propose a multidisciplinary approach using dietary restriction, exercise, and behavior modification in medical centers with the expertise to use all three techniques. Unfortunately, after I began my program, I ran into opposition from the federal government and medical insurance companies for the financial support of our program. Details regarding these projects are presented below.

Absorption of dietary proteins

My work (6-8) showed that the products of protein digestion in the intestine are amino acids, dipeptides (linkage of two amino acids), tripeptides (linkage of three amino acids), and tetrapeptides (linkage of four amino acids). These peptides, composed with the number of amino acids shown in the parentheses, are linked together with the peptide bonds. My studies showed that the theory of protein absorption as amino acids, which is published in all textbooks of physiology, is not valid because there is a large-scale absorption of di- and tri-peptides in human intestine. In fact, the absorption of the peptides is far more efficient than the absorption of amino acids. Furthermore, I found the existence of a peptide transporter that only allows the absorption of di- and tri-peptides. The clinical implication of my discoveries was that for feeding patients with reduced intestinal absorption, di- and tri-peptides, not amino acids, should be given as the protein source for the tube feeding. Using the techniques of molecular biology I found that there is nutritional and hormonal regulation of the population of the peptide transporter in the membrane of the cells lining the intestine. An implication of these studies is that the intestinal absorption of dipeptides can be upgraded or downgraded by nutritional or hormonal treatments. All of the above studies were supported by grants from the National Institutes of Health (NIH). Furthermore, in 1978 the American Gastroenterological Association used the picture shown below to introduce me to all of its members for the discoveries I had already made.

The American Gastroenterological Association used this picture to introduce me to its members.

Use of peptides for intravenous nutrition

After the above studies, I became interested in whether dipeptides can be utilized if given intravenously (9-10). This interest was motivated for improving the intravenous feeding of patients. For this procedure, usually amino acids were used as the protein source. However, the amino acids solutions are hyperosmotic and, therefore, must be infused into large deep veins in the body because in the deep veins the amino acids will be diluted in the large volume of blood and then are no longer hyperosmotic. This procedure requires expertise in the surgical technique of deep vein catheterization which sometimes causes problems. I proposed to replace the deep vein catheterization with the simple technique of putting a needle in a peripheral vein and using dipeptide solutions instead of amino acid solutions because dipeptide solutions are not hyperosmotic. To investigate the efficacy and safety of my proposal, I designed studies in subhuman primates (baboons) for testing. The baboons were denied any food by mouth for a month, but received their daily nutritional requirements by intravenous feeding called total parenteral nutrition. The protein source used was a dipeptide mixture. The baboons remained quite healthy and maintained their nutritional status without any side effects or complications. As a result I received worldwide patents for the use of dipeptides in parenteral and enteral nutrition.

The above results greatly interested the leaders of a company in Germany that specialized in producing intravenous nutrition solutions for patients. They proposed to perform clinical trials in patients needing intravenous nutrition in European medical centers. However, they argued that a complete dipeptide mixture, as we used in the baboons, would not be possible for the clinical trials because the cost of such a solution would greatly increase the cost of patient care. Until a technique can be found for a large-scale and cheap synthesis of dipeptides, they wanted to focus only on a couple of amino acids that can be added to the intravenous solution only in the dipeptide form. Glutamine is unstable in solution and tyrosine is poorly soluble. These problems can be avoided by using these amino acids in dipeptide form. They believed the addition of these amino acids would be of great benefit to patients.

The results of the clinical trial, which showed rapid utilization of dipeptides without any side effect, were submitted to the appropriate authorities in Germany and received approval for releasing a mixture of dipeptide and amino acid solutions to the markets in Europe. The above studies were funded by grants from several pharmaceutical companies.

Regulation of metabolism of branched-chain amino acids

The three branched-chain amino acids (leucine, isoleucine, and valine) are essential amino acids because the body cannot synthesize them and therefore, they have to be provided as daily dietary requirements. In fact, they form about half of the amount of required essential amino acids.

When I was a research fellow at MIT, I became interested in investigating the effects of diets on blood concentrations of amino acids. I found fasting as brief as one day increased the concentrations of all three branched-chain amino acids without increasing any other amino acid. To explain my finding, I found very little information available on the metabolism of these amino acids. Therefore, when I moved to the University of Pittsburgh, I organized a comprehensive research project, which lasted over 30 years, to investigate the metabolism of branched-chain amino acids and their regulation. For these studies I used human volunteers, experimental animals and their tissues, and cultured cells. To investigate the basic mechanisms of regulation, I used a variety of biochemical and molecular biological techniques. The following is a brief summary of my finding. When starved, both humans and rats increased their blood concentrations of branched-chain amino acids. This allowed us to use rats for determining which tissue was responsible for increasing the concentrations of the branched-chain amino acids. The results showed that it was the skeletal muscles.

To determine whether the reduced breakdown (oxidation) of these amino acids in fasting was responsible for their increased concentration in blood, I did the following experiment. I injected human volunteers with a trace amount of C^{14}-labeled leucine and measured the production of labeled CO_2 in their breath. I found that the catabolism of leucine to CO_2 was actually increased in fasting

To find an animal model for investigation of the biochemical mechanism of increased leucine oxidation in fasting, we used rats. I found that they do the same as in humans. Therefore I used rats to determine what tissue was responsible for the increased catabolism. The rat tissues were incubated with C^{14} leucine and the production of $C^{14}O_2$ (the oxidation marker) was measured. Between the two key tissues, the skeletal muscle and liver, only the muscle showed increased oxidation in fasting. I then investigated the effect of starvation on the steps involved in the breakdown of leucine. The first step is the removal of nitrogen from the leucine molecule and conversion to a ketoacid, which is the carbon skeleton of leucine. This step is under control of an enzyme named transaminase.

I found much greater transaminase activity against leucine in the muscle than in the liver. Furthermore, starvation greatly increased the transaminase activity in the muscle, but not in the liver. I then investigated the effect of starvation on the key enzyme regulating the breakdown of the carbon skeleton of leucine to CO_2. The activity of this enzyme, called branched-chain-ketoacid dehydrogenase, was also greatly increased in starvation. Finally, I found that several molecular mechanisms, like gene transcription and protein mass of the enzyme, are involved in increasing the activity of branched-chain ketoacid dehydrogenase (11).

In addition to starvation, I have also studied the effects of a variety of nutritional and metabolic alterations on branched-chain amino acids. These studies resulted in other laboratories also becoming interested in getting involved in this area of research. In fact, several suggestions for clinical applications have emerged. These include the use of leucine as the most potent amino acid: a) for stimulation of insulin secretion, b) for enhancing protein synthesis, and c) for treating hepatic encephalopathy.

On a personal note, because of many years studying leucine, I became so attached to it that I named my racing sailboat "Leucine." In return Leucine won me many trophies from the races at the Edgartown Yacht Club. I should also acknowledge that the execution of the above studies were assisted by many research fellows who were working with me.

Treatment of obesity

Although my preliminary result of treating obese patients with starvation while I was at the MIT Clinical Research Center was not encouraging, I did not give up my hope of finding a treatment. I thought it would be a major contribution to battling the most common health problem in this country. I had limited medical resources at my disposal at MIT, but when I joined the medical center of the University of Pittsburgh I had all the resources for putting together a multidisciplinary approach to the treatment of obesity. For example, I could use the expertise of dietitians, psychologists, and exercise physiologists. I asked them to design low-calorie diets, behavior modification techniques, and daily exercise programs for my obese patients. All of them individually had been previously shown to result in some weight loss, but never used all together as a comprehensive plan that I thought was necessary to succeed. The editor of the *Pittsburgh Post-Gazette* heard of my plan to treat obesity and sent one of his reporters to interview me. This lead to Marie Torre reading my interview in the newspaper and she promptly became interested to have me on her popular TV show. She was a television star of the Pittsburgh CBS and her program was largely to interview celebrities.

My TV interview was immediately picked up by the national CBS station and included in the national news because they considered the plan for treating obesity at a prestigious university medical center of great interest to the public. This resulted in my "fifteen minutes of fame" as an expert in the medical treatment of obesity.

A consequence of this fame was the telephone operators of my hospital were swarmed with telephone calls of obese patients requesting appointments to see me. The hospital director felt that I had a moral obligation to respond to the pleas of obese patients for help. He offered to convert a whole floor of the hospital as an obesity ward and provide me the faculties and staff that I needed to run the ward. I felt obligated to go along.

Initially, I planned that patients be admitted to the hospital to become adequately trained in my multidisciplinary plan of treatment and then to be followed in an outpatient clinic for long-term follow up. The hospital director ruled that the hospital cannot charge the patients for the cost of treatment because it is a university hospital. For people with medical insurance the company will be charged and for people without the medical insurance the Department of Public Assistance will be charged. A few short months after the opening of the obesity center, I got calls from the medical insurance companies and the Department of Public Assistance that they wanted to come for a discussion of my obesity program. When they came I gave them a tour of our obesity treatment floor and told them what we are doing.

They asked whether I had any proof that my treatment plan is successful. I told them it was too soon to tell. They responded that in this case they cannot financially support a treatment that has not yet been proven that it works. Furthermore, in view of the large prevalence of obesity, if they begin to pay for its treatment, they will become bankrupt. I argued passionately with them that many obese patients are suffering from serious complications and you are paying for treating these complications. If my treatment plan proves to be effective, the patients' sufferings could be prevented and you will be able to save a great deal of money. They were touched with my passionate defense of trying to treat obesity, but they would not change their position. After their departure the hospital had to close down my obesity center.

After giving up my medical treatment plan, I teamed up with the chief of surgery at Montefiore University Hospital to use a surgical treatment for massively obese (over several hundred pounds) persons with complications. The small intestine is the organ of nutrient absorption. My surgical colleague had developed expertise in reducing the absorption surface by cutting the small intestine below the stomach and then connecting the stomach to the lower part of the small intestine and closing the cut lumen of the cut small intestine. The operation was called the small intestinal (jejunal ileal) bypass. The operation was shown to be highly effective for losing weight. My nutrition team and I followed these patients after the operation. We were greatly disappointed when we found many of these patients developed serious liver disease that forced our chief surgeon to connect back the isolated small intestine to its original site. After this experience I published a review of our experience with the intestinal bypass operation and recommended that the procedure not to be used (12).

Finally, my research staff tested a series of natural compounds that we added to the rat diet in search of finding a "magic bullet" for reducing body weight. After trying a series of compounds, we found that a combination of pyruvate and dihydroxyacetone can do this. Unfortunately, when we tried the combination in obese patients, there was no effect.

After all these failures to find a cure for obesity, finally I gave up trying. My conclusion was that when obesity is established in a person it is almost impossible to reverse it medically. Therefore, all the efforts should be put to prevent it.

After I gave up trying to cure obesity, several medical centers began using gastric bypass surgery for the treatment of massive obesity. Apparently, the gastric bypass does not cause the serious complications of the intestinal bypass and can reduce weight.

The above accomplishments established me as a leader in the practice and science of medicine with a world-wide reputation. In a few short years after my arrival in Pittsburgh, I was promoted by the medical school to the position of Professor of Medicine with tenure.

Later, after the Heinz Foundation awarded a large grant to the University of Pittsburgh to setup research in the nutritional problems, I was also named as the University Professor of Nutrition. These recognitions were also the consequences of my being awarded several large research grants by the National Institutes of Health and by my prompt elections, as soon as I was nominated, to the two most prestigious medical societies, namely the American Society for Clinical Investigation (called the young Turks) and the Association of American Physicians (called the old Turks) and by my being well known and respected in the world of academic medicine.

14 Efforts to Advance Medicine in Iran

A major goal of Mohammed Reza Shah (the king of Iran) and his father (Reza Shah), the founder of Pahlavi dynasty, was to revive the glories of pre-Islamic Persia. Among the past glories was the creation of a world-renowned international university in Gundishapur, near the city of Susa in 271 C.E. during the Sassanid kings era (226-652 C.E.). The university had a large library (400,000 books) and a large faculty of international scholars teaching a wide variety of subjects with medicine being the most prominent one. There was a well-organized medical center under the direction of a medical director and a large medical staff, including physicians and pharmacists. This was the first of its kind

The former minister of the health, but then also the president of the Imperial Medical Center introducing me to the king.

in the world.

An admirable ambition of Mohammad Reza Shah was to revive the history by developing a medical center advanced in science and the practice of medicine which was modeled after the American National Institutes of Health (NIH). He saw a great need for this because many people from Iran and other Middle Eastern countries had to go to America for medical treatments or medical education. This was too far to go and far too expensive.

He hired American architects to design a city in the Northern Tehran to become the home of his imperial medical center. The financial support for building the medical center and its running expenses would come from his charitable foundation and the oil revenues. As the city was nearing completion, he asked his health

This picture shows the dinner party with the president of the Medical Center seated at the head of the table and my wife and I sitting next to him. Behind us, Dr. Robert Ebert, the legendary dean of the Harvard Medical School making a speech.

minister to put together an advisory board composed of the most distinguished leaders of American medicine. The minister, who had been educated in America and knew its medical leaders, recruited people like the dean of Harvard medical school and department chairmen from the University of California in San Francisco, Columbia University, and Yale University. For running the center the health minister asked my cousin, Dr. Homyune Kazemi, who was a professor of medicine at Harvard and the chief of the pulmonary division at the Massachusetts General Hospital, to serve as the dean of Imperial Medical School and asked me to serve as the Imperial Chief of Medicine.

During the 1970's, my cousin, Dr. Homyune Kazemi, and I, together with the advisory board, travelled to Tehran, Iran to open the Imperial Medical City and visit with the Shah and the Royal family. We were received in the king's private office in the Royal Palace. He spoke with great enthusiasm for his vision to make Iran a center of medicine for the Middle East. We were all very impressed by him and agreed to do whatever we could to help him to achieve his goal.

After meeting with the Shah the president of the Medical Center threw a celebratory dinner party in the most elegant private club in Tehran attended by the board of the Medical Center and my wife and me.

The advisory board put a great pressure on me and my cousin to move back to Iran as soon as possible and take charge of our positions. In fact, they even offered to come to Pittsburgh to help me pack for moving to Iran. My wife was very enthusiastic about moving to Iran because she liked the Persian culture and the beauty of the country and my sisters and close relatives showered her with warm reception. In addition, there were many Americans living in Tehran spreading the American culture and customs.

After my appointment as Imperial Chief of Medicine in collaboration with the President of the Imperial Medical Center and the dean, I began to develop an outstanding international medical faculty as my staff. We then went back to Pittsburgh to pack and pick up our children for relocation to Iran. As we were planning to move, early in 1979, unexpectedly, I read in the newspapers that there had been a colossal revolution in Iran forcing the Shah to flee the country. This was shocking and unexpected news to me.

When I was in Tehran visiting the Shah, I was so busy with affairs of the medical center that I did not have time to do intelligence on the political climate of Tehran. My impression of the Shah was that he was an unassuming, elegant, and generous person with sincere aspiration for advancing Iran to a level like Germany. As I mentioned in Chapter 5, my first meeting with the Shah was in 1950 when I was in the high school. He went out of his way to convince the government to exchange my Iranian money with dollars so I could come to America for my medical education. Furthermore, he was so impressed with my academic performance as a premedical student at Johns Hopkins University that he granted me a scholarship to cover the expenses of my going to four years of medical school. To cover these expenses in America with Iranian money would have been a great burden on my father's finances. However, I learned from the revolution that the Shah had two sides. There was one side that I personally knew and liked. The other side that I did not know was that during my years in America he had become a dictator to have absolute power. This resulted in an uprising of a large majority of Iranians who desperately wanted to have a democratic government. The people overthrew the Shah and brought back from exile the Ayatollah Khomeini, because the people thought he would be a holy and benevolent father to the nation. For a long time Khomeini had been a staunch opponent of the Shah and highly critical of his rule.

However, the move turned out to be a grave mistake. Apparently, people did not know that Khomeini had a different plan for Iran from being a father figure and a spiritual leader.

Khomeini made himself an absolute Islamic ruler and appointed a government with instruction to use Islamic rules to run the country (almost like the Taliban). The ruling Islamists hated America, and began to execute a large number of Western-educated people who had served in the Shah's government. The execution practice became so brutal that some of the senior Ayatollahs protested. These Ayatollahs were put under house arrest and the one who was supposed to be the successor of Khomeini lost his position. A large majority of Western-educated Iranians managed to escape the country and settle in countries around the world, particularly in the U.S. As a result the country lost forever its most valuable resource for advancing Iran to be among the developed nations.

I consider myself very fortunate to not have been in Tehran as the Imperial Chief of Medicine at the time of the revolution. Very likely, I would have suffered the same fate many American-educated Iranians working for the King did. I have more to say about this in the last chapter.

15 The Personal Impact of the Iranian Revolution

The news of upheaval in Iran greatly concerned me about the safety of my family living there because some had high positions in the Shah's government and most had completed their education in America. My sister Faranak's positions included an ambassadorial position in Turkey and the minister of education for Iran. She was also frequently invited to come to America for official meetings. My other sister was close to the royal family by being their fashion designer. Several of my relatives had high positions in the Shah's army. For example, my brother-in-law was a general and the father-in-law of my niece was a field marshal.

Some who were certain that they were doomed escaped the country, for example my mother's cousin, Manucher Kazemi, who was the minister of agriculture, by covering himself in a black chador pretending to be an Islamic woman. The ones who could not or did not want to leave Iran received serious punishments from the Islamist revolutionaries, including imprisonments, loss of properties, and even torture and execution. All of these actually happened to some of my relatives. I tried to persuade some family members, who were clearly in great danger, to come to America. I even got the assistance of my friend, the late Senator Jack Heinz, to get them visas or green cards, but for a variety of reasons they were not able to accept my invitations. My personal reaction to the

1979 Iranian Revolution is described in the last chapter.

As far as my own situation was concerned, I made the decision that as long as the Islamic extremists were running the country, I would never take a trip to Iran. As a former imperial chief of medicine, I could not risk getting into serious trouble with the Islamic extremists ruling the country. However, unexpectedly in 1998, I received a very friendly letter from the minister of health inviting me to Iran as a consultant to the Academy of Medical Sciences of Iran. Apparently as the result of the loss of many of their Western-educated medical specialists and scientists after the revolution, the quality of medical care and education had sharply declined. This greatly concerned Ayatollah Rafsanjani (president of the Islamic Republic) enough to ask his health minister to seek help from the Iranian medical experts living in America. Apparently, he also asked his ambassador to the United Nations (UN) to encourage the group of Iranians who were selected by the Minister to accept the invitation for coming to Iran. As a result I also received an invitation from the UN ambassador to come to a dinner meeting in his office in New York City. The reason for asking the help of the UN ambassador was that Iran did not have any diplomatic relationship with the US and therefore no regular ambassador.

After several days of thinking whether I should accept the invitations from the ambassador and health minister, I agreed to go to Iran. The most important reason was that the country of my birth needed my help and I could not refuse. The other lesser reasons were to see my family and to see what the Islamists had done to Iran. The next day, after I agreed to go, I received Iranian passports for me and my wife from the Ambassador's office in New York, something that normally takes several months to acquire. We had to have Iranian passports to enter Iran. It is mandatory that a person born in Iran, when entering the country, must have an Iranian passport. This law even applies to the wife and children that were not even born in Iran. I also knew that the US could not protect me in Iran if I ran into any trouble, because they had closed their Embassy there. I still vividly remembered the Islamic revolutionaries taking the members of the American embassy as hostages. Therefore, I had some concern about our safety on our first trip to the Islamic Republic of Iran close to 14 years after the overthrow of the Shah.

I lost my concern when we arrived in the Tehran airport and were treated with full courtesy and were rapidly processed through the passport control. However, when we entered the airport entrance hall, I could not hug and kiss my sister and also we were shocked to see that it was full of ladies covered under black chadors. This was quite different from our previous visits when we used to see ladies in the most colorful and fashionable Western dresses. Fortunately, my wife already knew the Islamic dress code and was prepared for it and complied with it.

Another new experience was our drive from the airport to my sister's house in northern Tehran. We frequently got stuck in heavy traffic, breathing very polluted air. However, when we got to my sister's house we began to experience a very pleasant life. The house was beautifully furnished, her servants were very polite and friendly, and everyone inside the house was wearing colorful and attractive Western clothing. They told us they can do whatever they like when inside the house, but when they go out, they must conform to the Islamic codes.

During my visit it was arranged that I spend my time at the two most important medical schools, one in Shiraz and the other in Tehran. When I arrived at the Shiraz Medical School, I was surrounded by the medical faculty with great enthusiasm. It appeared to me that they thought I had come from America to bring relief to their sufferings. They bitterly complained that since the revolution they had not been able to go to any medical conference in America or see any American medical textbooks or journals. They appeared to have been left in the dark about the recent medical advances. Their other bitter complaint was that their university salary had not kept up with inflation and the increasing cost of living. Therefore, they had been forced to work on jobs like being a technician in a laboratory at night.

I gave several lectures on medical advances in my field, all in English. Being away from Iran for so long and not speaking the Persian language had resulted in my inability to lecture in Farsi.

They assured me that the medical students and the faculty in the Shiraz Medical School all understand the English language. However, when I lectured in the Tehran Medical School, I spoke in Farsi. I had to do it because the Minister of Health asked me to do it. He feared that since there are Islamists among the students in Tehran, they might object to my speaking in English. To speak in Farsi, every night I had to stay up to translate my lecture into Farsi with some difficulty. Apparently, this gesture of mine was well received. However, I refused to conform to the Islamist dress code because I continued to shave every day and wear a tie, something that I have been doing since going to high school in Tehran during the time of the Shah. An example of my style of dressing when I was growing up in Tehran is shown on page 53.

On the last day of my visit, I met with the health minister and the president of the Iranian National Academy of Medical Sciences to discuss my plan of what I can do to help. I proposed developing an exchange program -bringing Iranian doctors to America for post-graduate specialty training and sending American doctors to Iran to teach medical students the art and science of clinical medicine. They appeared very interested in my proposal and promised to get in touch with me after they have gotten approval for the exchange program from the higher authorities. On departure they treated me very generously by paying all my travel expenses in American dollars.

After returning to Pittsburgh, I regularly checked my mail for several weeks for any communication from Iran. I became greatly disappointed that there was not any communication. I assumed that the hardliner ruling clerics objected to establishing any relationship with America because it might enhance the desire of people for seeking democracy and social freedom.

After my failed mission, I made several trips to Iran with the chief purpose of seeing my last sibling who had become old and not in good health to make the long trip to America. For my safety on these trips I avoided talking to any of the government officials or discussing politics with people outside of my family. However, without asking my sister or taxi drivers, they could not withhold their feelings of hatred for the ruling Ayatollahs and their miseries for living in Iran. My sister's death, three years ago, eliminated my desire for any further travel to Iran, especially as long as the Islamists rule the country and there is no democracy.

16 Life before and after Retirement

My life in America can be divided into two phases, one before and one after the retirement, because the two are radically different.

Life before Retirement

I had very little free time to relax and enjoy life's offerings when I was pursuing my medical studies or training. This pursuit, which started at Johns Hopkins and ended at Harvard and MIT, took about sixteen busy years, but enabled me to obtain both M.D. and Ph.D. degrees and fellowship training in gastroenterology and nutrition.

During this experience there were times that I could not even get the needed rest. For example, when I was an intern at Jefferson Medical College hospital, I was on call every other night, busy with medical emergencies. On my night off, I was rounding in my medical ward until late at night. This work intensity resulted in a life-threatening pneumonia.

When in 1966 I finished the medical-training period and entered the career-building period, my life became even busier than before. The responsibility for developing the first academic program in gastroenterology and nutrition at the University of Pittsburgh Medical Center demanded long hours of being at work. I had one leg in the hospitals seeing patients and the other one in my research laboratories to oversee my research projects. In fact, I got so behind writing my research reports and grant applications that I thought I should figure out a way to use my sleep hours to work on them.

Soon after I established my clinical and research programs at Pitt, because of the growth of my reputation, I began to receive many invitations to travel in the U.S. and around the world. They wanted me either to present lectures or serve as a visiting professor. I accepted most of these invitations because they allowed me to learn what was going on in my fields nationally and internationally.

My first memorable scientific trip was to travel to San Juan, Puerto Rico. Because malabsorption was a common problem there, the minister of health of Puerto Rico and his medical staff invited me to be a speaker at an international symposium on the intestinal absorption held at their medical school. I remember being invited to the palatial house of the minister for dinner. The house was located on the top of a high hill, which had a great view of the harbor. Furthermore, I was fascinated watching his staff roasting a whole pig on the fire to be served for dinner. I had never seen this before and never before eaten such delicious pork.

Puerto Rico was not too far to travel, but after that I had to travel to faraway countries like Australia and Japan. Nevertheless, when I got there I enjoyed the experience. In Australia I was invited to give the keynote speech at the annual joint meeting of the Australia and New Zealand Societies of Nutrition held in Sydney. After the meeting, my wife and I visited our friends who lived in Melbourne. We were charmed with the beauty of Melbourne and its surroundings, like Philip Island. This island gave us the experience of seeing fairy penguins returning home at night to feed their young after fishing all day in the southern ocean.

The trip to Japan also turned out to be a major and unforgettable event in our life. A former research fellow of mine, when he returned to Japan, became the professor of nutrition and the chairman of his department in Tokyo. He arranged for me to visit six universities in Japan to give lectures. It took two weeks to travel all over Japan to visit the six universities. In each visit we were warmly and royally treated. We liked the city called Kyoto the best. In this city we were entertained in a Japanese-style hotel (ryokan). We dressed in kimonos and sat down on the floor for a traditional Japanese dinner feast.

At the insistence of my wife after Japan we travelled to Thailand for her to learn Thai massage and to be introduced to Buddhism. From Tokyo we flew to Bangkok. For this trip I planned to stay in one of the most luxurious hotels in the world called the Oriental. For example, when we arrived around 2 a.m., the Oriental Hotel had sent us an elegant Mercedes with a chauffeur in a white uniform to pick us up. At the hotel we were treated like a royal couple. Our room was very large with beautiful furniture with fresh flowers everywhere. On the table in the sitting room area there was a very large plate full of all kinds of fresh fruits with a chilled bottle of champagne. We could ring a bell and immediately a servant would appear. From this experience I learned how the very rich travel and how they spend their wealth and decided not to repeat this again.

From Bangkok we flew to Chiang Mai and stayed in a guest house managed by a German family. When Joan was spending time in the Buddhist temple, the German owner of the guesthouse would take me on the back of his motorcycle to show me the countryside and primitive villages in the jungles of Thailand. The hill tribe natives appeared very poor, but very friendly. They insisted on feeding us the native food. Luckily, I did not get sick.

My travels became more frequent when pharmaceutical companies in Europe began their clinical trials on the use of the intravenous solution for the nutritional support of patients that I had invented. This required spending a week or 10 days every 2-3 months in Europe discussing the results. Most of our meetings were held in the Bavarian region of Germany in cities like Nuremberg, Erlangen, and Munich. I was put on a board of a foundation and was a lecturer in the Erlangen medical school. I got to know the Bavaria very well and became very fond of Franconia wine and sausages.

The next country to which I made frequent trips was Italy because I became a visiting professor in the Bari Medical School in the city of Bari. The chief of gastroenterology there, who became a very good friend of mine, would send members of his staff for research training in my laboratory in Pittsburgh. These doctors would then carry out our joint research projects in Bari.

Before going to Bari, I usually visited an Italian city most famous for its art treasures, like Rome, Florence, and Venice. The most unexpected experience of my travels to Italy was meeting Pope John. One day I was visiting the Sistine Chapel in the Vatican to see the art works and suddenly I saw Pope John in front of me.

I was speechless! All I could say was hello to him. It seemed that he was giving a personal tour of the Sistine Chapel to his Polish relatives.

Although visiting Florence was my ultimate exposure to art treasures, I found Venice one of the most charming cities in the world. The experience of walking in a city where there is no car traffic and looking at the old colorful and picturesque buildings lining the canals was unique among all the cities to which I have travelled.

The other countries that I visited for attending meetings were Sweden and Switzerland. In addition, I felt it was important to my research to take advantage of the above travels to   also attend pertinent scientific meetings or international congresses held in countries like England, Spain, France, Hungary, and the Czech Republic. Attending these international congresses enriched my experiences and knowledge of Europe. For example, in the East Germany I directly witnessed the suffering of people under the Communist rulers. I found the people had a very drab and unhappy life under the communists. This was made apparent when the East German professors were not permitted to come to my hotel to talk to me. In contrast, my trip to Hungary was far more joyful because the country just had been liberated from the communist rulers. For example, my wife and I were entertained in a gala reception in the presidential palace in Budapest and my wife greatly enjoyed going to an ancient public bath.

Because Hungary is close to Russia, we took advantage of our proximity and flew to Russia to visit our daughter, Jennifer, who was living there and had the mission of working on environmental pollution. Gorbachev had just taken power as the president. In spite of Russia being a superpower country, we were amazed to find the life there was quite backward, resembling that of third-world countries. It was difficult to find foods and other necessities. In short I did not enjoy my trip to Russia and have not gone back to find out whether the quality of life has improved since the dark days of communism.

In contrast to my trips to East Germany and Russia I always greatly enjoyed my professional trips to Spain, France, and

England. On a trip to Spain I ran into a situation which I had never experienced before. On my last night in Spain, I attended the farewell party of the minister of health of Spain in a beautiful museum in the city of Leon. The minister had arranged for an abundance of Spanish foods and drinks and had hired flamenco musicians and dancers to provide entertainment. I was having such a good time that I forgot that I had to take a flight back to Pittsburgh around 9:00 in the morning from the Madrid airport, which was over 200 miles from Leon. When the minister heard of my problem, he hired a taxi to drive me all the way from Leon to the Madrid airport. The drive was for several hours and after a couple of hours I developed an urgent need for urination. Because the driver did not know English and I did not know Spanish, I went through an unforgettable struggle to get him to stop near a bush so that I could relieve myself.

My trip to the French Riviera to attend an international scientific conference was another one that left me with a vivid memory. My hosts put me in the most elegant hotel in Monte Carlo with a great view of Monaco and in proximity to the most famous casino in the world. Although my modest gambling did not bring me any luck, I was greatly rewarded with meeting famous celebrities and movie stars like George Hamilton at the casino.

During the above travels a good deal of my time was spent performing. Therefore, my freedom was somewhat limited to allow me to enjoy the cultures or go see the museums or historic buildings. As soon as I arrived I was kept busy with an extensive itinerary. This included attending conferences, giving lectures, going to meetings, and socializing with the faculty members. However, most of my hosts allowed me some time to go sightseeing.

Therefore, I got to know a large number of countries, particularly in Europe.

The only memorable non-medical invitation I received was to participate in an international tennis tournament in Bermuda at the Coral Beach club. The invitation was by a famous and elegant tennis club. Several friends of mine who were members had proposed that I be invited. For a week I had great fun playing tennis and enjoying the offerings of the club like eating great meals. The last evening of the tournament the owners of the club invited us to their beautiful mansion for cocktails. After several glasses of champagne, I asked the hostess where they go for a get-away holiday while they live in such a beautiful resort. I became funny and said, "You probably go to Toledo, Ohio for a radical contrast." My impression of Toledo was that it is the most boring town I have ever been to. She looked at me with a stern face for a few seconds then said, "I am from Toledo, Ohio." Needless to say I have never used this joke again.

Most often the main intention of the invitation to serve as lecturer or visiting professor was to recruit me to join the medical school faculty of that school. Some of these medical schools were among the outstanding schools in the country, like the University of Washington in Saint Louis or the University of California in Los Angeles and the offers to join were generous. I could not bring myself to leave Pittsburgh because I had grown to like it as the "most livable city" and with great cultural and educational offerings. Furthermore, I had worked too hard and long to assemble an excellent group of coworkers to give up and go somewhere else and to start all over again.

The last big demand on my time occurred when the National Institutes of Health (NIH) asked me to serve as a member or chairman of the various committees. This was one honor that I did not enjoy very much because they sent me so many grant applications to review before traveling to NIH to present my opinions. Also, being locked up in a cheap hotel in Bethesda, MD, for several days was also not much fun. In view of the fact that NIH had generously supported the funding for my research projects, I felt obligated as a duty to serve.

Life after Retirement

As I began to approach the age of 70, I began to think of retiring. As a tenured professor it was up to me to decide whether I wanted to retire because, like the pope, my appointment was for life. In my decision I considered the following factors. First, I had everything I wanted in life, but very little time to enjoy them. For example, a 40-year record of well recognized contributions to the medical sciences, a wonderful family, two beautiful homes - one for the winter in Pittsburgh and one for the summer on the Island of Martha's Vineyard, toys like an antique sports car (MG) and sail and motor boats, memberships in The Pittsburgh Golf Club and the Edgartown Yacht Club for my winter and summer sport and social activities. Second, I had the good health to be able to enjoy all the above. I could not be certain how long my good health would last after the age of 70. This uncertainty was reinforced by discussion with my estate planner and wealth management people who seemed to think that I probably have less than 20 years to live. Therefore, if they are correct, I should close my medical career and start a life away from medicine with the centerpiece of spending more time with my family, especially my wife.

What have I done since I retired over 10 years ago?

More time with family

I no longer have to run to the office as soon as I wake up or come home late at night for dinner. Every morning before breakfast, when the weather is good, my wife and I go for a walk in the beautiful Chatham University campus that is one block away. After that we have a leisurely breakfast to discuss our plan for the day. At night we have a "happy hour" around 6:30 pm and then a leisurely dinner with a pleasant conversation about the news of our children and friends and plans about our cultural activities like going to the symphony, opera, and theater. We have some afternoons saved for the discussion of problems.

My wife and I have also been spending much more time with our three children and three grandchildren. Also I have become heavily involved in their job planning and finances.

Domestic Matters

I have learned to cook, like frying eggs in the mornings, making sandwiches at noon, and making salad and charcoaling or searing meat or fish at night. Other domestic matters that I have learned to do include help with food shopping and keeping our house clean. Doing the domestic chores have brought me pleasurable feelings that I have become a partner with my wife instead of expecting her to do all of the housework as some husbands do.

Edgartown Yacht Club
Wednesday Races – Rhodes Class
August 17, 2005

This photo shows me racing in my Rhodes 19 sloop
with the help of my wife as crew.

Pursuit of Sport Hobbies

I have spent much more time pursuing my sport hobbies like tennis, sailing, and biking.

This has resulted in greatly improving my skills in these sports. For example, I won the championship of the senior tennis tournaments of both the Pittsburgh Golf Club and the Edgartown Yacht Club. My summerhouse has become full of silver trophies for wining many sailing racing at the Edgartown Yacht Club. I'm shown above racing in my Rhodes 19 sloop with the help of my wife as crew. I usually need two crew members to race with one in charge of the jib and the other in charge of the spinnaker. In this particular race the use of the spinnaker was not allowed. Therefore, I needed only one crew.

My biggest fame in sports was to become known by almost all the people living on Chappaquiddick Island as the most enthusiastic bicyclist because every afternoon that I am not sailing they see me biking for several hours around the island. In fact, my close friend, the late Dr. Joseph Murray, who won the first Nobel Prize given to a surgeon for performing the first kidney transplant, used to call me Mr. Bicycle. This reputation resulted in a feature article on the front page of the *Vineyard Gazette* (13), the leading newspaper of the Martha's Vineyard Island, showing me riding a bicycle and a brief discussion of my life in America and my visions for peace in the world.

The above publicity has resulted in my becoming known by so many people on the Island of Martha's Vineyard. While I am biking, they frequently stop me on the road to talk to me. On many occasions, this has caused me embarrassment, because I cannot remember who they are while they seem to know me very well. Memory loss is one of the consequences of aging and I do not know of any remedy for it.

Travel for Pleasure

As I explained above, I took many trips to countries around the world, particularly around Europe, before I retired. All these trips were connected to my work and the host country had the total control of my time because they were paying for all my expenses. Therefore, I was not free to include very many pleasure experiences. Retirement allowed me to stop travel on business and travel entirely for pleasure. By paying my own expenses, I could choose the time, the place, and the travel plan as I pleased.

Initially I planned to travel in the winter to escape the cold weather in Pittsburgh and to go to places that were sunny and I could be physically active outside. For example, one year my wife went to Thailand to study Buddhism further. Since I had already been to Thailand and also was not interested to practice Buddhism, I joined a group of bicyclists to go biking around the islands of Hawaii. I was much impressed with its natural beauty of the several islands I visited. The most memorable experiences were biking to an active volcano in the mountains of the Big Island and going snorkeling.

Traveling from Pittsburgh to Hawaii took a long time; therefore, I decided to make shorter trips to explore the Caribbean Islands and the countries of Central America. For the Caribbean Islands we chose Puerto Rico, Bahamas, Virgin Islands, Barbados, and Dominican Republic. In Central America, we chose Mexico, Costa Rica, and Honduras. Our purpose in going to Mexico was mainly to see the ruins of the ancient Mayan civilization. We went with an American guide who was very knowledgeable about Mayan culture. We learned a great deal by spending several days in Palenque, an ancient site of the Mayan people. For example, we learned that they had no sympathy for the losers of their national tournament, which was throwing a big ball. The losers were sacrificed after the game. It is good that they vanished because very likely, like the pro-gun people in America, they would still insist that this is their Constitutional right to do.

To learn about the present Mexican Indians, we drove to Chiapas jungles. As we were driving a group of gun-bearing Mexican Indians stopped us. Our guide said they are rebels and want money for us to pass through their road, which we readily agreed to do. We found their villages very poor. In fact, they had no place for tourists to stay. We, therefore, had to set up tents to sleep at night. Our guide told us that the biggest cause of death in Chiapas is the bite of fer-de-lance snakes. This caused me enough fear to prevent me to go outside of our tent at night to urinate. Therefore sleeping at night in Chiapas turned out to be not pleasant for me. In the morning when I came out of our tent, I saw evidence of the visit of a wild animal around us, because I found that my Mexican straw hat that was hung on an outside pole of our tent was all chewed up.

The second Central American country we visited was Costa Rica. The main purpose of this visit was to go bird watching. With the help of friends who had travelled to Costa Rica and the travel book, we arranged our own trip. We reserved a lodge in Corcovado National Park, which provided us all our meals and an English-speaking guide with expertise in bird watching. We flew from Miami to San Jose, the capital of Costa Rica on an American airline, but when we arrived in San Jose, we had to take a Costa Rican airline that turned out to be a four-seater plane. The airport at our destination was a farm with cows and donkeys running around.

The captain seemed to have expertise in handling such a primitive airport. We found Costa Rica very beautiful and prosperous. We were impressed with their decision to spend their money on health and education rather than on the military.

The third and the last country we visited in Central America was Honduras. The main purpose of this trip was white-water kayaking in Honduras rivers. We took this trip with a group of professionals experienced in kayaking in Honduras. When we got there we found that there had been heavy rains raising the river water level quite high. This made the kayaking rather difficult requiring advanced skills that I did not have. Nevertheless, in view of spending great effort and money to get there, I felt obliged to try. Since in my first attempt I came near to drowning, I gave up kayaking in favor of exploring the jungles of Honduras. I found Honduras a poor country with a prevalence of diseases like malaria.

Our last trip in the American continents was south to Brazil. I debated for some time whether to visit Argentina or Brazil. Despite the fact that several professors in Argentina, who were previously my research fellows, had invited me to their country, I chose Brazil for the following reason. As an admirer of Theodore Roosevelt I read his memoir of his adventures in the Amazon in a book entitled River of Doubt. In fact, he almost died there, so I became curious to see what is going on in the jungles of the Amazon. We flew to Rio de Janeiro, which took us many hours. From there we flew to a small city in the Amazon called Manaus. We were surprised to find a great opera house in this small city in the middle of nowhere. We were told that a long time ago the robber barons were homesick for cultural entertainment so they built the opera house. In Manaus we chartered a riverboat to take us into the Amazon jungles. On our boat we had a staff of four: a captain, an assistant to the captain, a chef, and a guide. Our guide had lived in the Amazon jungle and knew its habitats and wildlife. After spending the day with our guide exploring the Amazon jungles, at sunset he would take us back to our riverboat for the night to have dinner and a comfortable bed, something that Theodore Roosevelt did not have. One night I insisted that, like him, I wanted to sleep in the jungle. The guide warned us of the presence of jaguar and deadly snakes in the near vicinity. He made us sleep in hammocks attached to trees. I found the hammocks not very comfortable for sleeping and did not ask again to sleep in the jungle.

With our riverboat we also visited several Indian villages in the Amazon. We found them poor and far away from any civilization. We distributed paper and pencils and candies to the children. They seemed to appreciate it. We returned back from Manaus to Rio de Janeiro for our flight back to the U.S. We stayed several days in Rio to see the city, to get together with a family we know, and for me to try to see the beautiful Ipanema girl that I keep hearing about in the songs on my radio. We enjoyed seeing the city and our friend, but I could not find the Ipanema girl. I think she is the fiction of the songwriter's imagination.

Besides winter trips we also took many trips in the spring. The main purpose of these trips, with a few exceptions like going to Alaska to explore the wilderness, was to visit our children and close relatives who were scattered all over the United States, Europe, and the Middle East. Our children were living in New York City, Boulder, Colorado, and San Francisco. Our close relatives were living mostly in Tehran, Iran, but some in Istanbul,

Joan and I on the Great Wall

Turkey; Munich, Germany; Toronto, Canada; and Golden, Denmark.

Among the above places we spent more time in Turkey and Iran because they had many more historic cities with thousands of years of civilizations. In Turkey we travelled from Istanbul, to Ephesus and Cappadocia. In Iran we travelled from the Persian Gulf in the south to the Caspian Sea in the north. We greatly enjoyed staying in the beautiful villa of my sister that was located on a sandy beach of the Caspian Sea. The caretakers of the villa prepared delicious dinners for us from the fresh fishes caught on her beach.

In Turkey we were entertained royally by my nephew and his wife's Turkish family. His father-in-law had the largest steel company, Borustan, in Istanbul and was a big supporter of art and music. From Istanbul we travelled to two of the most historic sites in Turkey: Ephesus and Cappadocia. Both places have played great roles in Christian history.

The aim of our recent travels has been to visit the ancient civilizations that had extensive interactions with the Persians. These include the Grecians, Romans, Egyptians, Chinese, and Indians. Before retirement, on several occasions, I spent time in Greece and Italy. Therefore, I did not need to go there. In fact, for several years I regularly served as visiting professor at the University of Bari in Southern Italy. After retirement one of my aims was to travel to the above countries that I had not yet seen.

A good friend who has founded a travel agency in Boston arranged for us to see the aspects of modern and old China. For me, seeing the old China was far more interesting than to see the modern China because I have seen many places like modern China in the U.S.

I was fascinated in Beijing by seeing the old imperial palaces and temples, the Forbidden City, the royal summer retreats and beautiful gardens, and certainly the Great Wall, which stretches 4,000 miles to protect China from foreign invaders. The trip to Xian was rewarding by seeing the statues of more than 7,000 life-sized terra cotta soldiers created to guard the first emperor of China in his afterlife.

The flight to the old capital of China, Chongqing, served to remind us of the American military presence in China during World War II by maintaining a museum of collections of American artifacts. It was delightful to see a big zoo that houses many beautiful pandas. Lastly, I learned that the historic and famous Silk Road began in Chongqing. The Silk Road, which went through Persia to the Black Sea, allowed trading between East and West and my ancestors played a great role in protecting the Silk Road through the Caucuses, which they governed.

In Chongqing we boarded a cruise ship to sail through the Yangtze River, which is the longest and the most picturesque river in the world, and to view the most spectacular gorges along the way.

After getting off the cruise ship, we flew to our final destination, Shanghai, which had many massive buildings which were left over from the European colonial era. However, I found the Shanghai museum to be the most impressive part of the city. The museum had the biggest collections of the Chinese arts like ceramics and calligraphy.

For a long time I was thinking about going to India, but I was discouraged by the length of the journey from Pittsburgh to Delhi. Finally, in 2013, I decided that before I get too old to travel I should make the trip. My interest for wanting to see India was based on the history of most profound interaction between Persian and Indian cultures for thousands of years. In fact, more profound interaction than with any other ancient culture I mentioned above. First of all, Darius, the great Persian king around 520 B.C.E. conquered India and made it part of the Persian Empire. This lasted for several hundred years and allowed both cultures to learn from each other things like writing books and playing games. For example, the Persians invented playing polo and the Indians playing chess. Secondly, in the 18th Century, a Persian king named Nader Shah was short of money to run the Persian Empire so he attacked India to bring back enormous amounts of gold and jewelry that are now stored in many rooms of a Jewelry Museum in Tehran, Iran. In fact, they support the Persian currency. In addition, Nader Shah also brought the famous and priceless Peacock throne of India to Tehran that has been used for several centuries for the coronation of the Persian kings. Lastly, for over a thousand years, from the 7th century to the 18th century, the Persians had enormous influence on Indian architecture and miniature paintings. For example, the most famous building in India, the Taj Mahal, was designed by a Persian architect. This influence began when a large number of Persians flew to India to escape the Arab invasion in the 7th century because they did not want to change their religion from Zoroasterism to Islam.

For our travel to India I did not wish to go as a part of a commercially organized tour. I wanted to have the freedom to

I am standing in front of the Taj Mahal.

choose where and when I wanted to go. It was lucky that I found an Indian travel agent in Pittsburgh who was willing to arrange for me whatever I needed. My needs were to have a private car, a chauffeur, and a knowledgeable guide who would serve as my personal staff. My other needs were to stay in hotels that were well-located and secured, had modern fitness centers, and could prepare my diets (no salt and low fat), and had digital communication centers for keeping in touch with my family and friends in the U.S. He assured me I could have all these in 5-star hotels in India. Indeed, all these needs were well met in every city we traveled to, but at a substantial cost. There is no direct flight from Pittsburgh to India. We, therefore, had to go to New York and from there to New Delhi. It took us over 24 hours to get there. The first city we visited was the old and New Delhi. The most impressive buildings in old Delhi were the Friday Mosque and the Red Fort both built during the reign of Shah Jahan, a Mongol emperor. Shah Jahan, which means the king of the world in the Persian language, was a descendent of the Mongols who had invaded Persia in the 12th century. After they were kicked out of Persia, they moved to India in the 16th century and established a dynasty there which lasted until the 19th century. They brought the Islamic religion and what they had learned in Persia with them to India. In New Delhi the most impressive building was the Palace of the British Viceroy of India. In the 17th century Britain's queen, Elizabeth I, granted the first trading charter to the East India Company. The East India Company became so powerful in politics and making money that in the 19th century the British government took over the country and made it a part of the British Empire.

From Delhi we went to Agra, the home of one of the most famous buildings in the world called the Taj Mahal, meaning the crown palace in Persian. The Taj Mahal was built also during the reign of the Shah Jahan in memory of his beloved wife. As I mentioned the architect was Persian.

From Agra we drove through Rajasthan to its capital Jaipur. The Mongol rulers had allowed Rajasthan to exist as a Hindu state under the rule of Maharajas. The Maharajas had built majestic forts and places for their elegant living and state governing.

From Jaipur we went to an old Indian capital called Aurangabad. The reason for going to this city was to make day trips to see two separate groups of caves. The first group was called Ajanta and they served as secluded retreats for the Buddhist monks. They were carved by hand out of deep curved mountains in 200 B.C.E. The caves were decorated with the treasure troves of numerous Buddha sculptures and ancient paintings. Ajanta caves fell into obscurity for more than a millennium when they were abandoned in 650 C.E. until 1819 when they were spotted by the British officers who were hunting for tigers in the area. The reason for abandoning the Ajanta caves was to carve out of stone new caves called Ellora to promote religious harmony. The caves of Ellora were built from 360 CE to 700 CE and belonged to people of three different faiths, Buddhist, Hindus, and Jains.

The last city we visited was Mumbai, previously called Bombay. The Persians, as immigrants, and the British, as a ruling class, had significant roles in the development of Mumbai as a great metropolis. There has been a colony of Persians living in Mumbai for several hundred years who have been successful as businessmen and philanthropists. As a result they are very much liked by the Indian citizens of Mumbai. In fact, in the center of the city, in front of the ornate municipal building, stands a tall statue of a Persian who was the mayor of Mumbai in the last century. Beneath the statue there is an engraved description that says he was "a great citizen, a great patriot, and a great regent." Not far from the statue there is a Zoroastrian temple built in the style used in ancient Persia, which admits only the members of the temple.

My plan for a future trip is to include Egypt, because of ancient interaction with the Persian civilization. In fact, Egypt was conquered by the son of Cyrus, the founder of Achaemenid dynasty around 520 B.C.E., but with the current political turmoil I do not think it is safe to travel there. I am also planning to visit Portugal to remind them that they once invaded Persia in the 16th century. The Portuguese, in search of influence in the Indian Ocean, conquered the island of Hormuz in the Persian Gulf. This island can be used to control navigations between the Indian Ocean and the Persian Gulf. At the time of this conquest Shah Abas, the great Safavid king, was the ruler of Persia. He did not have a strong enough navy to fight the Portuguese. He asked the British to use their powerful navy to expel the Portuguese from the Persian Gulf.

In February, 2015 my wife and I were encouraged by our friend Ambassador James Lowenstein, to go with him on a political tour of Palestine and Israel. As I have discussed in the review of history the area was once part of the Persian Empire and Cyrus, the Persian king freed the Jewish people from being slaves of the Babylonian people Furthermore, the Bible says that three Persian king came to Israel to honor the birth of Christ. Therefore, as part of my plan to visit countries that were part of the Persian empire, I was greatly interested to visit Israel even though I was afraid to go because of the hostilities between Palestinians and Israeli's. Ambassador Lowenstein assured me that we would be safe.

The political tour was arranged by an Englishman who had served as a foreign correspondent for the New York Times, who had previously traveled to Palestine and Israel and knew political leaders of both nations. Our itinerary was to visit West Bank's and Israel's major cities.

We learned a great deal from this experience. Gaza was excluded from our visit, because of Hamas. As recently as last summer there had been an outburst of a brutal war between Hamas and Israel. The political party of Hamas, who are the leaders in Gaza, still refuse after half a century to recognize Israel and continue to dream of driving the Israelis out of Palestine. Each time they have attacked Israel with their ineffective missiles they have received increasingly punishing responses from the Israeli Army. Clearly Hamas has been a major reason for the failure to establish peace between the Arabs and Jews.

During our political tour we had extensive discussions with the leaders of Israel and the West Bank. We also spent a great deal of time visiting people in their homes in both places. What we learned from these encounters would be too lengthy to describe. Therefore, I will discuss the key points of my observations.

People have a much better life living in Israel than in the West Bank. Initially the Palestinians in the West Bank were reluctant to make peace with Israel. Now they would like to make peace but the Israeli settlements are occupying most of their land. The peaceful demonstrations of Palestinians asking for freedom and their land is suppressed with brutal force. The ultra-conservative leaders of Israel would like all Palestinians to move out of Palestine and relocate to Arab countries. These people have remained as suffering refugees for several generations in the West Bank with the hope that someday they will be allowed to return to their homes and live freely. Some of the Jewish people we visited thought this would be possible if the leaders allowed it. Currently this does not seem likely. Finally, I was disappointed to see that

Joan and I in Jerusalem visiting the golden Dome of the Rock
where Prophet Mohamed was launched to heaven.

the Israeli conquerors of Palestine did not follow the policy of my Persian hero, Cyrus the Great, to be kind and tolerant to all religions and to allow the conquered people to live among the Jews.

Part 4: The Genesis of Animosity Between My Two Countries

17 Background

As an Iranian I am often asked my opinion about the behavior of the Iranian government toward America. This is a complicated question and cannot be answered in a few words and, in fact, I have to repeat some of the things that I have already mentioned. In the final chapter I will try to answer this question by a brief review of the historical background and the genesis of the present upheaval. For a detailed review I highly recommend reading the well-researched book of Stephen Kinzer entitled *All the Shah's Men* (14). I read this book a few years ago and still each time I read it I burn with anger about the secret and brutal mission of the CIA to Iran during the presidency of Eisenhower.

To begin with when I was growing up in Iran, the Iranians were great admirers of America and considered it as a good friend. This feeling was generated by the knowledge that in contrast to the European countries America has never become a colonial power and exploiter of the Middle East. They were impressed with the American generosity of helping many countries, including even Germany and Japan, to recover from the devastations of World War II. In particular, Iranians were grateful to President Truman for his financial support for improving their economic conditions and for his pressuring the Russians to remove their forces that were occupying Iran. As will be discussed, the good feeling about America disappeared after 1953 when America began a new policy of wanting to control Iran for its fear of communism.

After several thousand years of its existence, during the 19th century and the beginning of the 20th century, Iran fell into the hands of the most terrible kings they had ever experienced. These Ghajar kings were decedents of a Turkish tribe that had settled in Iran and had accepted the Persian culture. They all were absolute and corrupt rulers and incompetent to govern. Even worse, they began to sell Iran's important resources and the glorious relics of the ancient past to foreign countries, mainly the British. They used this money for their lavish expenses like the support of their harems with hundreds of wives and concubines and elaborate travels abroad, while there was great poverty and suffering in the country. Their army was so poorly trained and equipped that the result was the great territorial losses of the Persian Empire. For examples, the Caucuses were lost to Russia and Afghanistan to the British.

18 Over 100 years struggle for democracy

In mid-19th Century the wealthy families began to send their sons to Europe for their educations. These young men became greatly impressed with the prevalence of democracy in Europe. On their return home, they became active in awakening the people to the political and social freedom in Europe, which could remedy the situation in Iran. This was followed with a popular uprising of a coalition of intellectuals, merchants, farmers, and even the clergies against the king in 1906. The king agreed to become a constitutional monarch. A Parliament (Majlis) was formed with the task of drafting a constitution. The draft followed that of the Belgium constitution that was the most progressive in Europe. It put strict limitations on the royal power and gave the power of running the country to the members of an elected government approved by the Parliament.

After the establishment of the parliamentary governance, the king who had agreed to be a constitutional monarch suddenly died and a new Ghajar king came to power. The new king was firmly against the parliamentary governance. He got support from the religious leaders for abolishing democracy because they suddenly realized they would lose power by the secular form of the government and they wanted the country to be ruled by the Islamic laws. Encouraged by the support of the clergies the king sent his army to bombard the Parliament and arrest the deputies. In 1909 the constitutional forces from several cities marched to the capital and deposed the Shah and sent him to exile. They put his 16-year-old son, Ahmad Shah, who was quite immature, on the Persian throne.

To tackle the wide spread poverty, the Parliament, around 1910, voted to hire an American banker by the name of Morgan Shuster as the treasurer-general to stop the British and Russians from looting the Iranian resources and bring order to the financial management. This shows how the Iranians used to rely on

America for helping them against the two brutal colonial powers (British and Russian). In fact, a few years before inviting Morgan Shuster, the British and Russians had made an agreement between themselves to divide Iran into two zones of exploitations, north for the Russians and the south and east for the British. So it is easy to understand why the British and Russians got upset when the American came to help the Iranians. They ordered the Iranian Parliament to fire Morgan Shuster.. When the parliament refused, they sent their troops to encourage the young and immature Ghajar king, Ahmad Shah, to close the Parliament, which he did. This brought the "Persian Spring" of the constitutional revolution to an end in 1911. Afterwards there were several attempts to reopen the Parliament, but each time ending in closure. Nevertheless, Iran was the first Middle Eastern country that wanted to have a democracy like the countries in Western Europe. This was over 100 years before the recent "Arab Springs."

In the first decade of the 20th Century, oil was discovered in Southern Iran. In the second decade the British realized the immense value of this new resource. Winston Churchill (14) called it "a prize from fairyland beyond our wildest dreams." Using threat and bribing they compelled the young and impotent Ghajar king to sign the Anglo-Persian agreement that gave away full possession of the oil to England, with a token of annual income to Iran. The provisions of agreement also allowed the British to assume control over Iran's army, treasury, transport system, and communications. To secure their new power, they imposed martial law and began ruling by fiat.

The Iranians became outraged about what was happening to their country and the British realized that the county was about to fall apart by a widespread uprising. The colonial barons, under the leadership of Lord Curzon, the foreign secretary, got worried that in an uprising they may lose their gold mine in Iran. To protect it they decided that the weak Persian king should be eliminated and a strongman, who could control the natives, should be found and put in charge.

Speaking of Lord Curzon, it may be of interest to mention my involvement with his granddaughter when I was a medical student in Philadelphia. She came to Philadelphia to spend a holiday with a Philadelphia family who were friends of her parents in London. This Philadelphia family, who were also my friends, invited me to meet the granddaughter of Lord Curzon and take her out on dates. At that time I had not yet studied the history of the British takeover of the Iranian oil and did not know that Lord Curzon had a role in it. Therefore, I was delighted to take out and entertain the delightful granddaughter of the Lord Curzon.

Now to continue with my review of history, the British succeeded in finding the man they were looking for. He was a brilliant and tough military officer in the Persian Cossack Brigade by the name of Reza Khan. My father, who was also an officer in the Persian Cossack Brigade, knew Reza Khan very well. Both had fought together to prevent the country from coming apart. He respected the bravery and the nationalism of the Reza Khan. In fact, my father's recently published memoir describes his 30 years with Reza Shah in the army (5).

The British encouraged Reza Khan to overthrow the incompetent Ghajar king and take over the governing of the country. My father and a small group of Cossack officers planned a coup d'état to bring down the Ghajar dynasty and to install Reza Khan as the king. This was accomplished in 1926.

Reza Khan was a great improvement over any of the Ghajar kings by having great vision for securing and modernizing the country. These contributions, which are reviewed in Chapter 2, were overshadowed by him becoming a harsh dictator and an absolute ruler. He maintained a rubber-stamp parliament, because he did not allow free elections or speech. Although he freed social behaviors from the religious control, he showed no respect for the religious leaders that were helping people with their religious beliefs. However, he did have the courage to announce that he was going to cancel the Anglo-Persian agreement regarding oil, which horrified the British. They sent a clever and old friend of the Reza Shah to charm him with a phony offering of improving the agreement. Reza Shah fell for it and rewarded his old friend by adding 32 more years to the life of the agreement.

Later again Reza Shah began to dislike the British for their exploitations of Iran. To counterbalance this he established a friendly relationship with the German government. When World War II broke out, the British ordered Reza Shah to expel all the Germans from his country and break off his relationship with their government. He refused. This resulted in the occupation of Iran by the Allied Forces. The occupation ensured free oil for the British and also provided a convenient way to supply military equipment to Russia. Reza Shah was forced to abdicate and was sent to exile in a British colony in South Africa where he died.

The British also tried to find a descendent of the Ghajar kings to put him on the throne, but could not find anyone. They wanted to do this because they had an easy time with the Ghajar kings to get whatever they wanted. The British were then compelled to put the crown prince, the son of Reza Shah, on the throne.

The new king, Mohammad Reza Pahlavi, was educated in Europe and was quite familiar with the practice of democracy. Therefore, when he became the king, he allowed freedom of press and election to the Parliament. This enlivened the political mood of the Iranian people who had lived for more than a decade under the severe dictatorship of his father. The result was the blossoming of many newspapers representing a wide range of political groups, including the religious conservatives, nationalists, and communists. Without a doubt the most significant event was the reappearance of the greatest political leader that Iran has ever known. He was released after several years of exile and house arrest under the order of the Reza Shah. His name was Dr. Mohammad Mossadegh.

Mossadegh was born in 1882 to a very noble and wealthy family. His mother was a Ghajar princess and his father the minister of finance. He matured so quickly that at the tender age of 16 he was named to a government post as a chief tax collector. He received praises for his brilliant handling of his job, but personally he was horrified to see so much corruption and chaos in the Ghajar government. As a result he became one of the early activists for establishing democracy and reducing the power of the king in running the country. In 1906, when the popular uprising of the people succeeded in forcing the king to allow the establishment of democracy, Dr. Mossadegh was promptly elected to the newly formed Parliament to be a strong voice for the support of democracy. As I mentioned earlier, this Parliament was bombarded and closed by a subsequent Ghajar king. Mossadegh, realizing Iran was not yet ready for democracy, left the country to go to Europe for his education. He studied in universities in Paris and Switzerland. After getting a doctorate degree in Law, he returned to Iran. At the time of his return Reza Khan was rising in power and needed the talented and educated Mossadegh to help him to run the country. He had him serve as governor, finance minister, and foreign minister. The short and unhappy partnership ended when Mossadegh realized that Reza Khan did not share either his commitment to establishment of democracy or to the elimination of the influences of foreign powers. Therefore, he resigned his positions, ran for Parliament, and was easily elected. When he entered the Parliament, he found the deputies greatly in favor of selecting Reza Khan as a king (shah). Mossadegh was firmly and passionately against this selection. As the first Iranian popular political leader, he felt compelled to warn the deputies of Reza's authoritarian tendencies and predicted that elevating him to the throne would lead the country back to absolutism. He reminded the deputies of the many people who gave their lives in the constitutional revolution in 1906. Therefore, he would rather die than to agree to making Reza Khan the king. Despite the fiery speech of Dr. Mossadegh the Parliament voted for Reza Khan to become king. As Dr. Mossadegh had predicted, soon after the election, the Parliament was reduced to the role of a rubber stamp for Reza Shah, and he assumed the absolute power to rule Iran. To please the public, he tried hard to get Mossadegh to join his government. He offered him a high position, such as chief justice and even prime minister, but Mossadegh refused all the offers and continued to be the most vocal critic of the Shah. Reza Shah, fearing the popularity of Mossadegh among the people, felt he should silence him. Therefore, first he put him in jail, and then under house arrest.

19 Return of Mossadegh to Power

As mentioned above, Mossadegh was finally freed, after years of house arrest, by the successor to the Reza Shah. Soon after his release he ran for election to the Parliament and was elected with more votes than any other candidate. His strong voice once again began to thunder for the cause of democracy and elimination of the influence of foreign powers. A group of deputies became his disciples and formed a party called the "National Front" around him, which became the most popular party in Iran. My father became an enthusiastic supporter of the National Front Party. He knew the members and admired their visions for the future of the country. They asked my father if they could use our house for their private conference before each session of the Parliament. The reason they asked for our house was that we had the largest house just one block away from the Parliament. Our grand entrance hall with adjoining large reception hall was ideal for a large meeting. My father was happy to give them the permission to use our house and told us to stay away from the front of the house when they were meeting. I was very proud of my father to do this because as a teenager I wanted badly for the National Front Party to succeed. In fact, I took the position of being their host whenever they came to our house for their meetings. My father and I wanted Iran to have a real democracy without being anti-Shah. Our models were countries like England, Holland, etc.

The Parliament elected Mossadegh to be the chairman of its most important committee which was to oversee the oil policy. After long deliberations his committee decided to recommend the nationalization of the Iranian oil. The Parliament approved the recommendation. After the vote the deputies fell into deep silence because suddenly it occurred to them who the man would be with enough courage to inform the tough and powerful British of the Parliament's decision. This concern was based on the previous attempts of the Iranian government to negotiate a compromise on the Anglo-Iranian oil agreement. The British angrily rejected any compromise, including a 50%-50% division of the oil profits. In fact they threatened to use their military force to keep the oil agreement as it was, meaning the total possession by the British.

A photograph of the meeting of Truman and Mossadegh as reproduced from reference (15).

After some thinking the Parliament members voted to elect Mossadegh as the prime minister and as the man to confront the British. He was the most popular political leader and also known for his passion to free the country from the foreign exploitation of its resources.

The main reasons of Mossadegh to accept the offer of Parliament to become prime minister were two: one was to limit the power of the Shah to run the country and the second to nationalize the Anglo-Iranian Oil Company. He delegated the administrative functions of his government to my mother's cousin, the highly experienced Bagher Kazemi. Before becoming vice-premier, Kazemi had served for many years in various key governmental positions, such as foreign minister, under the two Pahlavi kings. Mossadegh put most of his energies to win his above two main objectives.

The only real remaining power of the Shah was his control of the army. With the massive support of the people, Mossadegh forced the Shah to transfer this power to the office of the prime minister and become truly a constitutional monarch.

For the second objective Mossadegh ran into the vicious

oppositions of the British colonial lords. Mossadegh argued that his country is poor and needs the income from the oil to improve the living conditions in his country. He offered to compensate the British for their investment in the Anglo-Iranian Oil Company. The British strongly opposed the right of Iranians to nationalize their oil, even with the offer of compensation. The British, like the present day America, resorted to using sanctions to prevent Iranians from exporting any of their oil to generate income. Furthermore, they froze all of the Iranian's deposits and assets in England. These harsh measures failed to deter Mossadegh from giving up his plan to nationalize the Iranian oil.

The colonial lords then took Mossadegh to the International Court in The Hague to retrieve their Iranian oil. The international Court ruled in favor of Mossadegh and his right to nationalize. The British then turned to their frequently used gunboat diplomacy threat to take back the Iranian oil wells by force. They sent 14 warships of the Royal Navy to the Persian Gulf and threatened to invade Iran. Fortunately for the Iranians, at the time of this threat the American president was Harry Truman and his foreign secretary was Dean Acheson. Both men were against the use of colonial power to milk the weak nations and deny them the right to establish democracy and improve their economic status. However, despite the position of the American government, the British went ahead for putting tight economic sanctions against Iran that worsened the already existing economic hardships. However, Mossadegh continued to hold to his conviction and did not abandon his rightful cause against all the terrible things that the British were doing to him, like taking their case to the United Nations to stop Mossadegh from preventing the British to own the Iranian oil. Actually, this resulted in Mossadegh becoming a hero to all the people living in the countries that were being ruled by the colonial powers. In 1951 Time magazine put him on its cover as the "Man of the Year," bypassing men like Truman and Eisenhower. In fact, Truman was delighted to entertain Mossadegh in the presidential guest house (The Blair House). As apparent from the picture shown below, Truman warmly greeted Mossadegh when he came to the White House to visit him. Mossadegh, like a large majority of Iranians, liked what America was doing for the world. Therefore, he thought that Truman would be supportive of his efforts to make Iran a prosperous and democratic country. Indeed, that was the view of Truman. Truman was not alone in his view because the members of the United Nations, when they heard the elegant and passionate speech of Mossadegh, voted in favor of Mossadegh's legal right to nationalize the Iranian oil.

20 America's Secret Destruction of Mossadegh

In the early 1950s England elected Winston Churchill as their prime minister. He was a great supporter of protecting the British Empire and was a ruthless agent of its colonial power. Meanwhile in America Truman was replaced with Eisenhower as president. During his presidency America was being lead into a serious paranoia about communism by Senator Joseph McCarthy. Also, the two most influential members of the Eisenhower cabinet were John Foster Dulles and his brother, Allen Dulles. John was the secretary of state and his brother the director of the Central Intelligence Agency (CIA). Both brothers before joining the Eisenhower cabinet had become fanatic anti-Communists. They did not even like nationalist world leaders like Nehru, who wanted to remain neutral in animosity between America and Russia.

The clever Churchill put aside his real motive that was to get back the Iranian oil and concentrated on convincing the Dulles brothers that Mossadegh was pro-Communist and consequently an easy prey for Russia to take over Iran. This cooked-up scenario was enough to frighten the Dulles brothers to fall into the Churchill trap that was to get them to agree to his proposal of overthrowing Mossadegh and abolishing his government. Actually the Dulles brothers had already decided to go after world leaders who seemed to them to be pro-Communist. The conniving Churchill set up Mossadegh as their first target. Later the Dulles brothers went after other world leaders (15).

As mentioned above, the Churchill proposal had been previously rejected by President Truman and by his secretary of state Dean Acheson. Initially, President Eisenhower was also against such a criminal proposal. In fact, he had already sent one of his personal friends to Iran to help the Iranian oil to flow again. Eisenhower initially also considered Mossadegh "the only hope for the West in Iran," precisely the view of President Truman before him (15). But in the face of pressure put on him by the two most ruthless colonialists (Churchill and his foreign secretary Eden) and by the two most fanatical anticommunist who were members of his cabinet (the Dulles brothers), he weakened and agreed with their plan. However, in his heart he knew that he was committing a serious crime because he told the Dulles brothers that he did not want to hear anything about their plan to destroy Mossadegh and his government.

It is hard to imagine that Eisenhower, who defended Europe against the atrocities of Hitler and was the man who warned us to be aware of the "military-industrial complex," would allow the Dulles brothers to commit a secret atrocity against a country that was a friend of America and seeking democracy and improvement of its economic condition. Unlike Truman, Eisenhower failed to see that he was brain washed into satisfying the great thirst of Churchill for the Iranian oil.

The Dulles brothers were overjoyed with winning the consent of Eisenhower and never bothered to find out who Mossadegh was and what he stood for. If they had bothered to ask anyone, like their CIA chief in Tehran, they would have quickly learned that Mossadegh was a descendent of a most noble and aristocratic family and a wealthy landowner. There was no possibility that he ever would be a communist sympathizer. In fact, all his life he had opposed the Russians attempts to get a foothold in Iran. The American chief of the CIA in Tehran wanted to tell them all these because he was firmly opposed to the American plan for a covert operation in Iran. Not only did the two Dulles brothers not listen to their CIA chief in Tehran, they actually fired him for trying to educate them. The CIA chief in Tehran was not alone in his opposition to the Dulles-Churchill plan because some of the most senior members of the State Department, like Ambassador Charles Bohlen, who had a good knowledge of the Middle East, also strongly opposed the plan of Dulles and Churchill to destroy the first legitimate and freely elected government that Iran had ever had for over several thousand years of its existence.

The CIA agent selected to be in charge of the covert operation was Kermit Roosevelt, the grandson of President Theodore Roosevelt. I do not know what really motivated Kermit Roosevelt to accept this assignment. I have been friends with several descendants of Theodore, including the son of Kermit Roosevelt, but I have been reluctant to ask any of them if they knew. Such a question might lead to an emotional argument and might possibly compromise my friendship with the Roosevelt family that I value.

Recently I discovered that Kermit Roosevelt, twenty six years after destroying the Iranian democracy, wrote a book entitled, *Countercoup.* I got the following impressions from reading this book (16). First, during his 1940's trips to Iran he became fond of Iran and its people, especially their king. Second, like the Dulles brothers, he believed the manufactured lies by Churchill that Mossadegh was about to lose the country to Communists. Third, he was a loyal subordinate of the Dulles brothers, especially Allen Dulles, and as a CIA agent he wanted to please them. Fourth, he believed Mossadegh wanted personally to replace the king with a coup, so Roosevelt was prompted to carry out the "Countercoup." This ignores the fact that Mossadegh was an old man and not in good health and the last thing he wanted to do was to become a king. He was satisfied with being Prime Minister. In addition, Kermit, like the Dulles brothers, ignored the facts that Mossadegh was chosen as the Man of the Year by *Time* magazine, gave a powerful speech at UN in support of his plans for Iran, and had had a warm reception by Harry Truman at the White House.

In view of what happened after his covert operation in Iran, Kermit Roosevelt was compelled to "sadly admit that what was a heroic story has gone on to become a tragic story (16)." I think Kermit and I both had a common ignorance of the Shah's having two sides. One side was his desire to make Iran a great country. The side we missed was his potential to become a strong dictator under the secret guidance of the American government.

Kermit Roosevelt was one of the most experienced CIA agents.

He secretly traveled to Iran with a suitcase full of American dollars to bribe the corrupt military officers, politicians, and senior clergies to do his dirty work. When he got there he met secretly with the king to tell him of his plan to overthrow Mossadegh. Initially, the king was afraid to agree with the Roosevelt plan, but after several secret meetings, he was persuaded to agree. This allowed Roosevelt to start his plan to bribe the corrupt politicians, officers, and ayatollahs to put together an army of hoodlums to go after Mossadegh. The first attempt was foiled and immediately the king, in panic, escaped the country. However, Roosevelt did not give up and organized the second attack that succeeded in overthrowing Mossadegh and his government. Roosevelt, in consultation with the Shah, who was hiding in Italy, appointed General Zahedi as the prime minister. This general had received a great deal of money from Roosevelt and therefore, had become a great fan of America. The general called the king to tell him that it was safe for him to return to Tehran.

21 America's Plan for the Shah

When the Shah returned, he had a meeting with Roosevelt to tell him how grateful he was to him and to America for making it possible for him to return to his throne. Initially, in 1941, the British put him on the throne after forcing the abdication of his father, Reza Shah. Now in 1953 he was being put on the throne for a second time but this time by the Americans. This resulted in transferring the king's dependency from England to America until the end of his reign in 1978; for over a quarter of a century he remained the most loyal and committed ally of America in the Middle East. He was instructed to become a strong ruler and to get rid of the communists and nationalists in Iran. It is a great shame and a great source of anger that Eisenhower did not instruct his ambassador in Iran to tell the King that for him to have continued to have American support he must become a democratic king and listen to the complaints and demands of his people. This would have prevented the bloody revolution of 1978 and the takeover of the country by the Islamic extremists. Instead, apparently, he was advised to assume full power and clear the country of people opposed to the throne especially the Communists.

As a result the first thing he did on his return was to punish Mossadegh, whom the Dulles brothers called a "mad man," and his cabinet members. He put Mossadegh in prison for several years and then under house arrest until the end of his life. He exiled his vice premier, who was my mother's cousin, to an awful place in Southern Iran to suffer greatly. Furthermore, he ordered the execution of Dr. Mossadegh's foreign minister. The Shah then took full control of the army, the Parliament, and the judiciary with no more free press and elections. He executed a great number of people like the army officers loyal to Mossadegh.

I am certain that the leaders of the American government, unlike Churchill, did not care much about the Iranian oil. Their real purpose was to develop a strong military leader in the Middle East to prevent the spread of Communism, which they greatly feared. They saw this opportunity to use the Shah of Iran for this purpose. They seduced him by giving him advanced military equipment and a promise of becoming a nuclear power. Furthermore, with the assistance of the CIA and Israel they helped the Shah to create a most efficient secret service (Savak) necessary for his operation as a strong man. All these American efforts succeeded in converting the Shah from a democratic leader to a most repressive king. When I was a teen-ager living in Iran, he appeared to me to be trying to be democratic by allowing free press and not controlling parliamentary elections. The only vestige of power he wanted to keep was to control the army, but Mossadegh disagreed and took it away from him.

After Mossadegh was put in prison, his dream of nationalizing the Anglo-Iranian Oil Company was abandoned. In its place an international consortium was organized to harvest the Iranian oil. The major share was given to American and European oil companies and a minor share to Iran. Under the Shah the income from the oil was mostly used to buy expensive military equipment from America. . This was a great mistake, because Shah should have used the oil income to eliminate the prevalent poverty and to improve the economic status of low-income families. This was in part the main goal of Mossadegh. The Shah's other mistake was his rapid westernization of Iran, ignoring that a large population of Iranians were conservative Moslems. Like his father he paid very little attention to the wishes of the religious leaders, like Ayatollah Khomeini, who consistently criticized the Shah's policies. Instead of listening to him Shah sent Khomeini to exile in Iraq. From there Khomeini began a campaign to bring down the Shah. Finally, the severe repression and poor economic policies resulted in a widespread uprising of the people against the Shah. Initially, he used his military forces to stop the uprising, but after a great deal of bloodshed, he realized that he had no choice but to compromise. But by then it was too late for a compromise because an overwhelming majority of the people had become determined to abolish the monarchy. All he could do was to find the old national front party members of Mossadegh and to ask them to take charge of the country and leave for abroad and never to return.

22 The Fall of Shah and Rise of Moslem Clergy

Soon after the King's departure, Ayatollah Khomeini returned from exile. There was a massive outpouring of people to welcome him, because they believed a holy religious man had come to save them from tyranny and repression. He cleverly called the revolution Islamic despite the participation of many non-Islamics, like the nationalists and the seekers of democracy.

For me personally this was a great tragedy because, as a Persian and proud of my ancient heritage and of my family serving long lines of kings, I wanted Iran to remain a kingdom. At the same time I had come to the firm opinion of wanting a democratically elected prime minister to run the government and a king to serve as the guardian of democracy, an arrangement as in England.

Also personally, I greatly liked the king and was grateful to him for all his generous contributions to my plan to become an accomplished and internationally recognized professor of medicine. I also greatly liked his vision and efforts to revive the pre-Islamic culture and social traditions. To me it was a great tragedy that he succumbed to the temptation of becoming a dictator and against democracy. It is a shame that no American president, besides Harry Truman, ever tried to advise him that he should become a democratic king because he was a loyal ally of America. In fact, all the presidents for over a quarter of a century, after 1953, wanted the king to spend the oil income to buy American arms and be their strong man in the Middle East.

As I have already discussed, I met Mohammad Reza Shah in his royal palace in 1950 when I was a teenager. I found him to be a very kind and caring person and highly intelligent. He went out of his way to help me and my friends to go abroad for our education. My picture with him appeared on the front page of the leading daily newspaper in Tehran. Right after my meeting with the Shah, I came to America to study medicine. I became very busy with my studies and also was not kept informed of what was going on politically in Iran. I remember hearing that Mossadegh was overthrown as the prime minister by his opposition. Nothing was mentioned about the roles of America and the Shah in this personally distressing news. In fact, I became aware of the criminal action of the U.S. government many years later in 2003 when Stephen Kinzer published his well-researched book entitled *All the Shah's Men* (14).

The second time I met Mohammad Reza Shah was in the 1970's when I went to Iran accompanied with a group of most distinguished leaders of American medicine who were medical advisors to the Shah. The group, particularly the dean of Harvard Medical school, put pressure on me to accept the offer of the Shah to become his "Imperial Chief of Medicine." They argued that as a Persian, I had an obligation to accept the Shah's job offer.

The day after our arrival, we met with the Shah in his palace. I was again very impressed with his vision to develop a city of medicine in the north of Tehran, to have a first class medical school, hospitals, and research programs with the promise of all the necessary expenses to be paid by the Pahlavi Foundation that was under his control. The only concern I had was whether the Iranian leaders of medicine would approve of my appointment. During my visit to various medical schools in Iran, everyone I met appeared enthusiastic about my taking the position.

In my brief visit I did not have time to find out about the popularity of the Shah and his government. From talking to the members of my immediate family, I learned that they were happy with the advances under the Shah and they all liked their jobs working for him. One of my sisters was the secretary of education and the other was the fashion designer for the royal family. My brother was the head of the pharmacy department in a major hospital and my brother-in-law was a commanding general in the army. My wife was also spoiled with the shower of attention she received in Tehran and became enthusiastic about moving there.

A little while after we returned to U.S. and were preparing for moving to Tehran, unexpectedly I received the news that there had been a bloody revolution in Iran and the Shah had been deposed and had left the country. I was stunned with the news and began to worry about my family in Tehran. Luckily, I could reach them by phone. They assured me they were alright and were hiding in their houses and had quit their jobs and had destroyed all the things that connected them to the Shah such as letters, medals, and pictures. I asked whether they wanted to move to America. They said it would be very difficult for them, especially in absence of having any money in an American bank and also abandoning their friends and relatives and homes and settling in a new country in their advancing age.

Shortly after the departure of the king, Ayatollah Khomeini returned from exile and life in Iran radically changed. In sharp contrast to the people's expectation that his return would usher in a new era of freedom from dictatorship and respect for human rights, totally the opposite occurred. Unknown to most of the people, he had an entirely different plan for Iran.

He wanted the Islamic clergies, like himself, to be the supreme leaders and to rule the country under the strict Islamic laws.

The supreme leader, always a member of the clergy, could not be questioned or challenged, but always must be obeyed because he speaks for God. This was Khomeini's idea, because neither prophet Mohammed nor the Koran mention anything about a clergy running the government. As a result of Khomeini's great desire for power and control, people not only lost all traces of democracy, but they also lost all the social freedom that they had enjoyed under the Shah, for example wearing any clothing they liked, being romantic in public, having alcoholic drinks, or eating any pork products. In fact, social and sexual indiscretions by women became punishable by stoning to death.

Under Khomeini Iran lost a great treasure, which was the highly educated or skilled people, by either killing them or forcing them to emigrate. These included people who had served under the Shah, people who were educated in the West and people who were not Moslem. As a result the country lost its thousands of years character as a plural society and suffered a great "brain drain." The killing was so massive and thoughtless that the deputy and successor to Khomeini, Ayatollah Montazeri resigned from his job. Khomeini was the first hard-core Islamist militant in the history of Islam and became a model for others to follow.

I should emphasize that I have respect for all religions including the Moslem religion, but I strongly believe that religion and governing should be kept separate. I am not alone in my belief, because in my travels in Iran I have heard from the taxi drivers saying that they are devout Moslems but do not like the mullahs running the country. Furthermore, history provides strong support for my belief, namely that civilization in Europe did not greatly advance until religion and governing were separated.

Now the answer to the question of why there is a bad relationship between the Iranian and United States governments. It all began with the fanatic anticommunist Dulles Brothers believing the phony accusation of Churchill that the popularly elected and democratic prime minister of Iran was pro-Communist. In 1953 they ordered the CIA to overthrow Mossadegh and put back on the throne the Pahlavi king. After the overthrow, for more than a quarter of a century, the American government became the mentor of the Shah of Iran and supported him in becoming a harsh dictator. This relationship ended in 1979 when there was a violent and bloody revolution against the Shah forcing him to leave the country.

Khomeini held America responsible for keeping the Shah in power who was violating the Islamic laws and had very little relation with the Islamic establishments. He became fearful when he heard that the American president, Jimmy Carter, had allowed the Shah to move to America instead of sending him to Iran for prosecution which Khomeini had requested. He thought once again, just like in 1953, that America would put the Shah back on the throne against the will of Iranians. In response he encouraged his hard-core supporters to take over the American Embassy and its diplomatic members as hostages. This was followed by many demonstrations against America with people shouting "death to America." This animosity grew even further when America became a supporter of Sadam Hussein, the president of Iraq, who had attacked Iran with his weapons of mass destruction (toxic nerve gas) killing nearly a million people of Iran. All of these together lead to the formation of Moslem jihadist terrorists in other countries that were determined to hurt American people.

I am greatly concerned that the American political leaders do not seem to have learned any lesson from the consequences of their 1953 action in Iran. President Obama has put many severe economic sanctions against Iran and is threatening military action. He seems to have forgotten his promise of his first election that he will try to solve the problems with Iran peacefully and by negotiations, and not by any hostile approach. Now that he is elected for a second term, he does not have to listen to the hawkish politicians and can do what is best for America. There is an abundance of evidence that military actions have not helped us to resolve world problems, for example, many years of wars in Vietnam, Iraq, and Afghanistan.

Actually, in these wars America lost a great number of its soldiers and a great deal of its money without achieving any victory. These losses are minor compared to what could happen if America attacks Iran. Compared to Iraq and Afghanistan, Iran has a much bigger population and a much stronger and better-equipped army. Therefore, the cost of attacking Iran will be much greater. Although I would be happy with a regime change in Iran, I think the people living there should do this. Furthermore, I think a wise approach to cool off the hostile relationship with Iran is to stop the sanctions and the threat of war and enter into a nonthreatening dialogue with the newly-elected president, Hassan Rouhani, who seems eager to establish a cordial relationship between the two countries. We should do this even if we do not like an Islamist government in Iran because many Iranians, especially the educated ones, are eager for a friendly relationship between the two countries. In the past we maintained a cordial relationship with the Soviet Union and China even though we did not like the Communists to rule their countries.

At the present the only Moslem country that does not have a religious warfare among its citizens is Iran. Furthermore, the Iranians might be willing to help us to fight the Islamic extremists to bring political stability to the Middle East. It may be hard to believe, but, as in the past, the only country in the Middle East that likes America is Iran. You will find this if you travel among Iranian people. Therefore, I believe it is to our interest not to allow the current negotiations to fail.

Not well known publicly there was once a possibility of resolving the hostile relations between the two countries and the United States sabotaged it. This happened about a decade ago when Khatami became the president of Iran. He was a moderate cleric. He declared publicly that he was interested in opening a dialogue where each country could respect the other. In fact, his government began to cooperate with the US military in fighting the Taliban in Afghanistan. Suddenly our bullish president, George W. Bush, in the State of the Union speech before Congress, labelled Iran as "an axis of evil." This accusation gave ammunition to the Islamic extremists, who hated American, to attack Khatami. They criticized him for being foolish to think that he could have any kind of cooperative relationship with the American government. Therefore, the Iranian overture for resolving the hostility was promptly discontinued. In addition to the above foolish act, the policies of George W. Bush, in my opinion, have led to the unleashing of the present religious warfare in the Moslem countries.

The Iranian negotiators claim that they plan to use nuclear power for peaceful purposes and not for making bombs. All I know is that for over 300 years the Iranians have been peaceful by not attacking any other country. However, the Iranian negotiators need to be assured that United States and its ally Israel have given up any plan for a military attack against them. In return, they need to provide sufficient evidence that Iran has also given up any plan to develop nuclear bombs. The reward for such an agreement will be to allow Iran to join Western countries for economic development and trade. The Iranians desperately need such an agreement to stop their economic sufferings.

The United States was the first to develop a nuclear bomb. Shortly afterwards the technology spread to other countries, such as Russia, England, France, Israel, North Korea, Pakistan and India. To protect our world there should have been greater efforts than the Non-Proliferation Treaty. There should have been efforts instead to abolish ALL nuclear weapons by all of the above countries. It is a hypocrisy to concentrate efforts prohibiting one country from building a nuclear bomb when other countries are allowed to keep theirs.

On occasion, I have been asked why I am concerned about my country Iran's having nuclear bombs, because so many countries have it. My response has been that if Iran develops nuclear bombs, it is likely that other countries in the Middle East would follow suit. With the serious animosities existing between different peoples, such as the Shiites and the Sunnis, this may have serious consequences.

23 Post Nuclear Accord

My book describing the history of animosity between Iran and America was published in June, just before the two countries reached an agreement on nuclear bomb making. This became the hottest political issue of the summer of 2015 and a major source of debate in our Congress.

It was therefore a great relief when President Obama succeeded in convincing the members of Congress that the agreement must be approved because there is no better alternative. In late summer of 2015 this resulted in the majority of the Democratic senators voting approval while all of the Republican senators remained opposed. The Republican senators ignored the fact that our five major allies had already approved the agreement and were busy establishing relations with the government of Iran.

If we had disapproved the agreement, the following consequences would have occurred. First we would have become a lonely power in the world. Second, the nuclear accord would have been nullified and the Iranians could have proceeded with making nuclear bombs.

The fact is that we desperately need to bring peace to the Middle East. There is currently a crisis in Europe about what to do with the millions of desperate refugees risking their lives to escape the Middle East. Normalization of our relations with Iran may help our crisis, but this requires our taking the initiative because of the following reasons: Presidents from Eisenhower to George W. Bush have committed a series of criminal or hostile acts against Iran. The Iranians must be assured that these acts will not be repeated. These acts have been described in detail in Chapter 22 but are repeated and summarized here.

- In 1953 the US secretly sent a CIA agent to Tehran to destroy the government of Dr. Mossadegh, the most beloved and respected prime minister that Iran has ever had and a true nationalist. John Foster Dulles, the Secretary of State under Eisenhower, who ordered the attack, did not care that the consequences of his action would be to kill the Iranian dreams of democracy and prosperity that were being achieved under Mossadegh. The US committed this crime because Foster Dulles was greatly influenced by Winston Churchill's belief that Mossadegh was pro-Communist. Churchill was mainly interested in getting back control of Iranian oil and Dulles was only interested in destroying an alleged pro-Communist leader.
- Promptly after destroying Mossadegh government, the US committed the second atrocity by putting the King (Shah) on the Persian Peacock throne and supporting him for a quarter of a century as an absolute ruler. This resulted in a bloody revolution. The Shah was overthrown and forced into exile. The country fell

into the hands of the Moslem extremists with terrible consequences.

- During the 1980's the US government, during the presidency of Ronald Reagan, wished to punish the Iranians for having taken members of the embassy staff as hostages. This was done by encouraging Saddam Hussein to attack Iran, which he did. He used toxic nerve gas to kill over half a million Iranians during eight years of intense fighting. It is not well known that the hostage taking and the demonstrations calling "death to America" were the revolutionaries' response to the actions of Jimmy Carter. Against the advice of his staff, he invited the king to come to America. The Moslem rulers feared that the US was planning to repeat the 1953 plan, namely to restore the king to this throne. After they became convinced that Carter did not have such a plan, they returned all of the hostages without harm.

- In 1988, in a case of mistaken identity, an American naval ship shot down an Iranian passenger plane (Iran Air) in the Persian Gulf, killing three hundred innocent passengers.

- In 2003, Khatami, a moderate Iranian president, got the courage to declare publicly that he would like to have a civil and respectful dialogue with America to resolve the animosity between the two countries. He went even further towards reconciliation by secretly sending the Iranian army to help American forces in their war in Afghanistan. Unexpectedly, George W. Bush in his State of the Union address labeled Iran as an "axis of evil." This sadly destroyed the tenure of Khatami as president. The Islamic extremists criticized him severely as a fool to hope to have friendly relations with America and brought to power a ruthless Islamist named Ahmadinejad.

- Several years ago Iran began a program of nuclear enrichment. This became of great concern to the US and its allies. The Iranians claimed it was for peaceful purposes, but the US did not believe them. As a result, the US and its allies imposed severe sanctions against Iran, causing great economic hardship and isolation.

It must be realized that the nuclear accord was only the first step to begin the long process of bringing into alignment the differing goals of the two countries. The next step is to start removing sanctions in the next few months if the United Nations' inspectors find no evidence of the nuclear bomb making in Iran. Then we must begin establishing formal diplomatic relations with Iran, including trading ambassadors, as we do with our other world allies. These ambassadors must work on harmonizing our interests in the Middle East with those of Iran. There is already some agreement between the two countries regarding foreign policy. For example, both countries do not like Al-Qaida, the Taliban or ISIS.

The Republicans view the Iranians as terrorists and not trustworthy. This viewpoint, as I discussed in a recent issue of the Pittsburgh Post-Gazette (17), is not helpful in resolving half a century of animosity between the two countries. The severe sanctions and resulting isolation have not proved helpful to our foreign policy. Therefore, the time has come, to do just what we have done with Cuba, to initiate a new approach with Iran.

It has been reported that over 60% of Iranians are under the age of 30, so they are too young to remember or care about the upheavals of the past. In fact, they are anxious to see how the approval of nuclear accord is going to bring them peace and friendship with America. They expect to be allowed to come to America, to participate in our culture, and to get advanced training in science and technology. Furthermore, American and Iranian business men have been waiting for an opportunity to interact with each other.

It is unrealistic to expect immediate changes in the behavior of the Islamic rulers. The older Iranians have already gone through two revolutions to bring back democracy and each time they were massacred by the military agents of either the king or the Islamist rulers. Therefore, they have given up this approach. Instead, they are counting on the release of sanctions, coming out of isolation, and mixing with the people of the Western world to bring about a gradual change in their system of government and hopefully the eventual return of democracy.

Conclusion

In conclusion, looking back to over 64 years ago and remembering my feeling for wanting to come to America, the following thoughts come to mind. First of all I would like to give credit to myself for the great act of courage for traveling alone as a teenager, without having ever travelled to a foreign country and over a distance of the half of the world (between Tehran and Washington) requiring over two days of flying in a non-jet airplane and without being able to speak English. Among the many countries that I could have gone to for my medical education, I chose America because all my consultants told me it was the best place for my purpose and I wanted to get the best medical education. Actually, my father pleaded with me to go to Sweden because it was much closer to Iran than America and, therefore, much easier to come home for a visit. Secondly, my cousin was the ambassador to Sweden and he had offered to look after me if I went there.

Reading American history, I became a great admirer of Thomas Jefferson and Abraham Lincoln. Prior to reading American history, the only person I greatly admired was Cyrus the Great, the ancient Persian king. All the above three men were the greatest supporters of human rights and freedom. I thought the American constitution was a gift of the founding fathers who were most remarkable visionary men. Unfortunately I became disillusioned in my feelings for America when I learned of the secret atrocity committed against Iran during the Eisenhower presidency. More recently I have been outraged by the ill-advised and bullish policies of George W. Bush, who dragged us into war with Iraq and Afghanistan. Apparently, he was either ignorant of or did not care about the history of these countries. In the 1920's Iraq was attacked by the mighty forces of the British Empire under the same slogan that we have come to bring democracy, but after great losses, they could not wait to get out of there. More recently, the forces of the superpower Soviet Union attacked Afghanistan and paid a heavy price without gaining anything.

In face of the many disasters that we have experienced in

wanting to police the world, we should give it up and give this role to the United Nations. This requires getting the members of the U.N. to agree to participate in a unified force to keep the peace in the world. We should promise that we will help the U.N. action if a large majority of the members are in agreement and would cooperate. We should also promise to be a moral, but not a military, leader for the world and if our resources allow, help poor or suffering countries.

References

1. Metz, Helen Chapin, (Ed.). (1987). *Iran: A Country Study.* Library of Congress. Federal Research Division.
2. Daniel, Elton L. (2001). *The History of Iran.* Westport, CT: Greenwood Press.
3. Polk, William R. (2009). *Understanding Iran.* New York, NY: Palgrave Macmillan, a division of St. Martin's Press.
4. F.S. Farmarfarmarian (2009), Georgia and Iran: Three Millennia of Cultural Relations (1-43), *Journal of Persianate Studies*
5. Memoirs of Sadegh Adibi entitled *30 Years with Reza Shah in the Army* had been published in Farsi language by Nashar Alborz, Tehran, Iran (1385 Persian year).
6. Adibi, S. A. (1980). Role of small intestine in digestion of protein to amino acids and peptides for transport to portal circulation. In M. Winik (Ed.), *Nutrition and Gastroenterology* (pp. 55-75). Hoboken, NJ: John Wiley and Sons, Inc.
7. Adibi, S. A. (1983). Amino acid and peptide absorption in human intestine: implications for enteral nutrition. In G. L. Blackburn, J. P. Grant, & Young, V. R. (Eds.), *Amino Acids: Metabolism and Medical Applications.* Boston: John Wright.
8. Adibi, S. A. (1997). The oligopeptide transporter (Pept-1) in human intestine: biology and function. *Gastroenterology,* 113, 332-340.
9. Adibi, S. A. (1989). Glycyl-dipeptides: new substrates for protein nutrition. *Journal of Laboratory and Clinical Medicine,* 113, 665-673.
10. Adibi, S. A. (1997). Renal assimilation of oligopeptides: physiological and metabolic importance. *American Journal of Physiology,* 272 (*Endocrinology and Metabolism* 35), E723-E736.
11. Adibi, S. A., Harbhajan, P., & Vazquez, Jorge A. (1992). The metabolic basis for increased oxidation of branched chain amino acids in starvation. In P. Schauder, J. Wahren, and R. Paoletti, et al. *Branched-*

chain Amino Acid: Biochemistry, Physiopathology, and Clinical Science (pp. 69-82). Raven Press.

12. Adibi, S. A. & Stanko, R. (1984). Perspectives on gastrointestinal surgery for treatment of morbid obesity: the lesson learned. *Gastroenterology*, 87, 1381-1391.

13. On his bicycle Siamak Adibi ponders peace. (2006). *Vineyard Gazette*, 161 (17). Photograph.

14. Kinzer, S. (2003). *All the Shah's men: An American Coup and the Roots of Middle East Terror.* Hoboken, NY: John Wiley & Sons, Inc.

15. Kinzer, S (2013),*The Brothers: John Foster Dulles, Allen Dulles and Their Secret World War.* Times Books, Henry Holt and Co.

16. Roosevelt, Kermit (1979), *Countercoup: The Struggle for the Control of Iran.* McGraw Hill Company.

17. Adibi, Siamak (October 15, 2015), *The US Should Compensate Iran for Interfering in '53.* Pittsburgh Post-Gazette, Vol. 89, no. 76

48541767R00096

Made in the USA
Charleston, SC
05 November 2015